Buddhism:
Tools for Living Your Life
Vajragupta

Windhorse Publications

Published by
Windhorse Publications Ltd
169 Mill Road
Cambridge
CB1 3AN, UK
info@windhorsepublications.com
www.windhorsepublications.com

© Vajragupta 2007
First published 2007
Reprinted 2008, 2011

Cover design by Marlene Eltschig
Cover Image: Wooden Spoons © Royalty-Free/Corbis
Printed by Bell & Bain Ltd, Glasgow

British Library Cataloguing in Publication Data:
A catalogue record for this book is available from the British
Library

ISBN: 9781 899579 74 7

contents

about the author

Vajragupta was born Richard Staunton in 1968 and grew up in Bromley, London. He studied psychology and sociology at Aston University, and first came in contact with Buddhism in Birmingham in 1990. He was ordained in 1994 and given the name Vajragupta, which means 'secret, or hidden, diamond-like truth'. He was director of the Birmingham Buddhist Centre from 1997 to 2005, and teaches Buddhism and meditation at classes and retreats across the Midlands.

Vajragupta enjoys nature and wild places, and also loves gardening, poetry, and the visual arts.

acknowledgements

There are so many people who have taught me about Buddhism. There are many others whom I have taught, and whose questions, insights, and experiences have given me a deeper perspective on the material I've presented. This book has arisen from many years of such sharing of understandings and attempts to practise a spiritual life. There are quite a few people who may recognize themselves in a comment or anecdote found in these pages.

I'd like especially to thank five friends: Geoffrey Moorhouse saw a very early version of the manuscript and gave advice and, most of all, encouragement when it was most needed. Kalyacitta and Roy Peters have given much of their time, feedback, suggestions, and encouragement. Saddhanandi also made some very helpful comments on an earlier draft. Jnanasiddhi at Windhorse Publications has helped me turn a rather scrappy manuscript that had a few good ideas in it, into something more presentable. At each stage of the process she has been able to point out what needed to happen for the text to improve. I've learned a lot and I am very grateful. Finally, Shantavira (also of Windhorse Publications) has edited the book in meticulous detail and saved me from dozens of tautologies and typos, misnomers, and mixed metaphors. His careful work has significantly improved the clarity and the flow of the text.

preface

I was a young man in my early twenties when I first stumbled across Buddhism. I was just completing a university degree, but I had no idea what I wanted to do next. The prospect of the future frightened me. I felt confused, unsure of myself, and full of a sense of life's futility. Although I was studying psychology, it seemed to teach me very little about who I was and how best to live my life.

I started going along to Buddhist meditation classes. I didn't have any big 'meditation experiences' in those early days, but something kept me going. What the Buddhists said made sense, and their approach seemed pragmatic. They were, I felt, seriously and genuinely attempting to live a life according to their values. They weren't just people with well-meaning ideals, but trying to work out what those ideals meant in practice. They were warm and friendly, and I felt no pressure on me to conform. I had a sense that I was 'coming home'.

I gradually got more involved in Buddhism until, one day, I knew that this was what I wanted to do with my life. I realized I was a Buddhist, that it was this vision of life and its possibilities that made most sense to me. I was eventually ordained within a Buddhist order, or spiritual community, and ended up teaching meditation and Buddhism at the place through whose door I had first ventured years ago – something I would never have dreamed of back then.

I am still teaching at that Buddhist centre, and I've seen many more people pass through that door and test for themselves the practices and teachings of Buddhism. Many of their stories and their reasons for wanting to explore Buddhism are different to mine, but there are also similarities, and the same questions and issues crop up again and again.

In this book I have attempted to convey a feeling for what a 'Buddhist life' might be like – the underlying flavour, or ethos, of such a life. I hope I have made it clear that this way of life is possible for anyone – whatever their background and experience. My aim is to make the teachings as accessible and relevant as possible, and to give you some 'tools' with which to live a spiritual life.

Each chapter describes some of the basic principles, and then explores how we can implement them within our own lives. I've tried to keep my approach as 'nuts and bolts' as possible, with plenty of examples of how to put the ideas into practice and anecdotes about people's attempts to do this. There are also several exercises and reflections which you are welcome to try. Their purpose is to help you consider how you yourself might put a given ideal, or method, into practice. I hope to encourage you to think about your own situation in the light of the topic under discussion.

The book is structured in a way that tries to anticipate the kind of issues that arise for people when they first encounter the teachings of Buddhism, and as they gradually become more involved. So the first chapter begins by exploring the kind of questions that might get us interested in Buddhism in the first place, what it is that might motivate us to seek out a spiritual path.

The following three chapters look at some of the practical methods Buddhism offers for finding answers to these questions, and for bringing about the personal growth and development that this entails.

A big issue often arises at this point: is it really possible to make use of these tools for self-transformation when your life may already be quite full and busy? Chapters 5, 6, and 7 look at spiritual practice in everyday life, and the support we need in order to sustain it.

Then, we might have noticed Buddhists doing rituals, chanting, or bowing to a shrine. We may wonder why they do this, as we've heard there is no God in Buddhism. Chapter 8 considers myth and ritual from a Buddhist point of view.

The following three chapters look at the Buddhist life on a deeper level – that of developing wisdom, seeing through to the truth of reality. We look at how the Buddhist life is one of constant reflection upon our experience and the world around us. Again, the emphasis will be on practical methods for reflection. We also look at how wisdom manifests as compassion: a desire to help alleviate the suffering in the world.

Another big question for many people who encounter Buddhism is its teaching on death and rebirth. What do these mean, and does one have to believe them in order to practise the Buddhist way? Chapter 12 addresses this topic.

The final chapter looks back at the ground we have covered and then looks ahead to where the path might lead if we continue to pursue it, by asking what the ideal of 'Enlightenment' might mean.

Because the book provides a general survey of a Buddhist way of life, it necessarily covers a lot of ground in a relatively short space. There is much more that could be said about any of the topics in this book, and plenty more complexity and subtlety involved in trying to put any of them into practice. In this book I have introduced the fundamental principles, given basic instruction in using the main tools or practical methods, and, I hope, given something of the flavour of Buddhist practice – enough to get you started. To help you explore further, you'll find some suggestions for further reading in the endnotes.

The book is written primarily for those who are new, or fairly new, to Buddhism and Buddhist practices such as meditation. However, some of the material, especially in the middle and later chapters, may also be of interest to those who have more experience.

four reminders

everyone has a story

To write down all I contain at this moment
I would pour the desert through an hour-glass,
The sea through a water-clock,
Grain by grain and drop by drop.[1]

Everyone has a story to tell. Everyone's life is a unique combination of events, full of dark and light, hope and disappointment, meetings and partings, the unusual and the mundane. Living a Buddhist life is about understanding our story, knowing for what our heart most truly wishes, and feeling we have the tools to change direction if we wish. Life will have dealt us a certain hand of cards, but we can learn to play them more and more skilfully.

In the Buddhist communities I've been part of, we would often tell each other our life-stories. Each person will take an evening, maybe longer, and tell the story of his life thus far. Over the years I've heard many stories, and each has been intriguing, even inspiring. There is no such thing as a boring life-story.

As a result of hearing their history, you usually feel you know that person much better. This greater understanding allows you to feel more empathy with them. Maybe you can see that they arrived in the world with a particular physical and psychological make-up already in place. They were also born into certain family, social, and cultural conditioning. They tell how they juggled with this complex, interacting set of conditions, and how they struggled to find happiness and fulfilment in the midst of it all. You hear of the long course of chances, circumstances, and choices that brought them to where they are to-day. What they describe helps make sense of the person you now know. You can see where they have come from. You can recognize them in the story they tell.

I once saw an exhibition of photographs that consisted of shots of the same objects close-up and from a distance. A photograph of a tree would show a tangle of twigs and branches twisting and pointing in different directions. The next image would be a long avenue of trees – each one beautifully proportioned and in line with all the others. Another photograph would show a heap of stones of various shapes and sizes, the weathering and the lichen giving each a different colour and texture. The next picture would be the same stones from afar – a wall of regular width and height that ran alongside a road, perfectly following every curve of the road and contour of the hill.

Our lives, too, can be like this. Close-up, day-to-day, there is just a busy jumble of incidents, conversations, and experiences. Only from a distance can we discern an overall order or pattern. This is partly why going on a retreat can be so valuable – we can look back at our lives from a distance. We can take stock and consider whether we are head-ing in the right direction. Are we going where we really want to be go-ing? Are we becoming the kind of person we really want to be?

The Buddhist life involves asking those kinds of questions. Buddhist practices, such as meditation, are about becoming more aware, or con-scious, of the patterns of our lives. Through the Buddhist life, we try to become more consciously the authors of our own life-story. We are trying to ensure that life is not something that just happens to us, but increasingly an act of creativity. This means not only creativity of the artistic kind (though it might include that), but that we engage in all aspects of our lives with fullness of attention and purpose. We are aware that each little incident will become part of the larger narrative of our lives.

One great danger of the today's busy world is that life can slide past us without our really noticing it. How often have you eaten a meal, made a journey, or even had a conversation with someone, and afterwards realized that you weren't really there, and that your mind was caught up with anticipation or worry about the next thing? Although, in the western world, life is often enjoyable and comfortable, there is a danger of superficiality, of living too often in a twilight zone of distraction.

I have a friend who, at the age of twenty-one, witnessed her younger sister dying of cancer. Her sister was only sixteen, on the cusp of an adulthood she would never live. As the months wore on, the family looked after her as best they could – managing trips to the hospital, washing and feeding her increasingly sick and frail body. Their lives revolved around being there for her in those last weeks of her life.

It is a tragic story, yet my friend says there is something about those days that she has been trying to recapture ever since. In some respects the aim of her Buddhist life is to live the way she lived then. The family lived in the presence of death. They knew the sister would not be around much longer, but this enabled them to be much more alive for her and for each other. Every moment of every day was precious. Of course, they did not always manage this perfectly, and there were occasions of anger or irritation, but they gave themselves to the situation, they had a tremendous sense of being fully present.

Eventually the young girl died, the funeral came and went, and life for this family gradually returned to normal. My friend says that part of the pain of this subsequent period was the loss of the depth and presence they had all lived with. She couldn't sustain that intensity of awareness of life under ordinary conditions, but she had been left ever since with a sense of its potential.

Maybe we, too, desire to live more fully, more from the depths of ourselves. When we manage to do this, life seems somehow more real, more authentic, and therefore more satisfying – even if we are in the midst of pain and suffering. We realize that we have often been living as shadows of ourselves, existing as a fraction of our potential. We are capable of much more feeling and awareness than we dare to imagine.

sacred questions

When we look back on our lives, the pattern may seem obvious to us. We might have been quite conscious of our intended direction from early days, or it might have seemed meandering and stumbling. But maybe we still sense that there was something we have been gradually working our way towards. This something compels us, drives us on, without our quite knowing why. Even if we try to ignore it, it keeps coming back, reminding us of its presence.

exercise – *life-story*

First, spend some time reflecting on your own life-story. One way you can do this is to get pen and paper and make a storyboard of twelve pictures. In other words, choose just a dozen key phases or incidents of your life, those that have been most influential and given your life direction.

Create the storyboard in words or, if you like, simple pictures. The point is not to produce a work of art or anything polished. It is just to get you thinking!

You may find yourself choosing events that somehow symbolized a time in your life. (For example, on my first night at university I found myself with a group of students who, to my dismay, were talking only about how much money they expected to earn when they graduated. For me, this one incident encapsulates a strong aspect of my experience of that time of my life: one of disappointment and not quite fitting in.)

Secondly, take some time to reflect on this story. Are there themes or patterns that you can see in your life, questions that consciously or unconsciously have been trying to work themselves out, or aspects of yourself wanting to express themselves?

Jack Kornfield, a well-known Buddhist teacher, has described how, becoming more conscious of this compelling force in our lives, we can formulate what he calls a sacred question – a question that summarizes what it is we are searching for.[2] Our sacred question might be existential: we wonder what life is about, whether it has any meaning, and what happens after we die. Or the question might be of a more psychological nature. Perhaps we want to know why we are so restless or anxious, or low in self-esteem. Or, for us, the question might be about relationships: how can we understand others more deeply and love more fully? It might be a question about the state of the wider world: is there anything that can be done to relieve the suffering we see around us? Or again, it may be that we had psychic or meditative experiences when we were younger, experiences that still seem significant to us and that cause us to wonder about our lives now. Or we might be drawn by a sense of beauty and potential.

I have a friend who, as a young man, in the days before he was a Buddhist, was travelling in Thailand. One evening, out for a walk, he turned a corner and came across a serene Buddha statue. Tears suddenly welled up in his eyes. He could not stop looking at this beautiful figure, for he had seen an image of the peace that he really wanted in his life.

As each of us has a unique life-story, each of us may have a different sacred question, a different reason for being drawn to the path of self-transformation. We will only be spurred on to this path, and find a sustainable route along it, by the question that burns for us, not necessarily by those that are urgent to other people. We will only be really motivated to seek answers to the questions that are most crucial to us.

exercise – *your sacred questions*

Returning to the reflections on your life-story from the exercise above, can you formulate something that is a sacred question for you?

Again, start by sitting quietly and allowing time for your thoughts and feelings to emerge. It would also be good to use pen and paper, but what you write doesn't have to be polished or complete. Sometimes such questions evolve gradually. To start with, you may get just a faint sense or intuition of what it is that matters most to you. Or perhaps you already have a very clear idea.

Just express your question (or questions) as clearly as you are able.

I had a strange experience the first time I went on retreat, which has never happened again since then. I was a student at the time and had very little money, but I wanted to go on a Buddhist retreat. The group retreats at established retreat centres cost more than I could afford, but I'd heard some Buddhists talking about 'going on solitary'. A solitary retreat is when you stay on your own somewhere in the country-side and spend your time meditating, reflecting, going for walks, and reading. I knew of a caravan in Wales, in an ideal location, and very cheap to rent, so I booked myself two weeks there. It was in a beautiful spot halfway up a steep hillside. Just a few yards from the caravan were stunning views to the sea. Every evening I would walk a short distance and watch the sun setting into the Irish Sea. I would probably have been better off doing my first retreat at a centre where someone more experienced could provide some guidance, but nevertheless I gained a lot from being on my own.

At the beginning of the two weeks, without my consciously deciding to, I started thinking through my life. I found myself spontaneously recalling a certain period of time, memories would come flooding back to me in meditation, and even in my dreams I would be remembering people and incidents from the past. By the end of the fortnight I realized I had reviewed my whole life and that it had happened roughly in chronological order. Through this process I came to know and accept myself more fully. I felt tangibly more confident and sure of my direction when I returned. It was a pivotal time in my life, a life-changing two weeks.

I realized that all my life I had been looking for something. I had not found it yet, but I knew that, through the Buddhist practice I'd learned, and through my contact with other Buddhists, the search had truly begun. After many years of wondering what my life was about, I was on a path at long last. On one of the final evenings of the retreat, the sunset was particularly lovely, the sea calm and silvery, and the light from the sun made a red pathway across the water. It was as if I was setting out on that pathway, setting out across the ocean towards that beautiful sun.

the four reminders

We've seen that the Buddhist life involves having an ongoing sense of the story of our lives and being aware of what is really important and vital to us. It means being more alive to the opportunities for realizing that significance and possibility. But it is very easy to lose touch with all this, as the earlier story of my friend and her sister shows. Through the busyness, distractions, and comforts of modern life we can slip back into our 'default setting'. Our old habits reassert themselves, and we trundle through life without really addressing our deeper questions. Because of this, it can help to have some practical tools to ensure we don't forget our true potential and purpose.

The rest of this chapter concerns a set of reflections from the Tibetan Buddhist tradition that are designed to help us cultivate and keep alive this awareness. Traditionally known as the 'four thoughts that turn the mind towards the Buddhist teaching', they have also been called the four reminders, because of this need to keep reminding ourselves to make the most of our lives.[3]

exercise – *the four reminders*

What follows is an explanation of the main idea behind each of the four reminders. Then there is a more reflective evocation of each one. Try reflecting on these over the next few weeks.[4]

There are more practical suggestions about how to carry out reflection in Chapter 9. For now, you could reflect on one reminder for five minutes each day. This could be at the start of your meditation – if you already have a daily meditation practice – or it could be at another time, while sitting quietly or going for a walk. You first need a space free of distraction, some time being quiet and getting settled, and then you can start the reflection.

You could focus on one reminder for a week or so, and then move on to another. Or you could rotate them on a daily basis, doing a different one each day.

The basic idea is to mull over what it is we are being reminded of, and to notice what, if any, effect that has on us. You could slowly read the relevant reflection to yourself a few times. Or you might know another piece of writing, a poem, or a song, a piece of music, a painting, or a photograph that addresses the same theme. Just let the main message sink in to your heart. There is no need to try to force any response – keep it simple and trust your intuition.

The idea is that, through sitting quietly and contemplating the four themes, they gradually drop down more and more deeply into your being. At first, your reflections may seem a bit abstract and artificial, but, with practice, they gradually become more emotionally real, and become part of you.

You could even keep a journal, briefly recording what impression each reminder makes upon you.

1. life is a precious opportunity

The first reminder is that life is a precious opportunity. Just the fact of being alive is extraordinary. Notice what you can see, hear, taste, touch, and smell right now. Even the sound of a car going past, or the smell of a flower, is a miracle. We can remember the past and imagine people and places in the future. We can communicate with others. Even if life is currently difficult and painful, at least we do have life and awareness.

For most of us reading this, it is likely that we live in a prosperous place in the world and a favourable time in history – a time and place of unprecedented wealth and freedom. We can bring to mind all the material things from which we benefit.

What else is there in our lives to be grateful for? There may be our family and friends, all the riches of the culture we've grown up in (art, books, films, music – imagine life without any of them), even the spiritual teachings that have been helpful to us. Are there other 'blessings' you can think of, anything or anyone that has enriched your life?

We can also consider whether we sometimes take life for granted. Do we sometimes waste our opportunities?

> *I'm alive and aware.*
> *How extraordinary this is!*
> *Today I will see so many forms and colours, hear so many sounds.*
> *I can think and feel and use my imagination.*
> *How amazing to be alive.*

> *I have food, shelter, money, and all the basic necessities of life.*
> *Many people in the world are not so fortunate.*

> *I have family and friends, people who care for me.*
> *We can communicate and talk – what a wonderful thing!*

> *There is so much natural beauty in the world.*
> *It is all around me every day.*
> *There is also art and music, culture and education.*
> *There are spiritual teachings that inspire.*
> *There is so much of value in the world.*

> *Do I make the most of these treasures?*
> *Do I appreciate the precious opportunity of life?*

2. impermanence

The second reminder is that of the truth of impermanence. Life may be precious, but it is also fleeting. In this reflection we simply bring to mind the fact that everything in this world will pass, and we are no exception.

As we get older it seems that the years pass by more quickly, we gradually become aware that life is running out. The point of this reminder is not to make us morbid, but to instil a sense of urgency, to get us to remember what is really important while we still have time. In a sense, life is precious *because* it is fleeting. We must make the most of our opportunity.

There is a popular saying, 'When you die, your in-tray will still be full.' We can spend so many of our days rushing around trying to deal with what is in that tray, but it is never-ending, and how much of it is really that important? If we knew that in six months our lives would end, would we be so concerned with its contents? Or would we have different priorities – people, family, and friendships? When reflecting on this reminder we can consider all these kinds of questions.

An old aphorism says, 'Live life as though today is your last, but as though it will last for a thousand years.' In other words, to have a sense of urgency does not mean rushing headlong into our lives, but living from a sense of spaciousness in which we can see what has real meaning and importance. Does this aphorism suggest anything to you about how you live your life?

> *Everyone who has ever lived has also died.*
> *Countless numbers of people have been born and passed away.*
> *This will happen to me too.*
> *One day I will have to face death.*
> *I can never know when this will be.*
> *It could be tomorrow, or next week, or next year.*
>
> *All my friends and family, too, will pass away.*
> *In a hundred years from now, we will all be gone.*
>
> *Life is fleeting, so I should remember this.*
> *It is good to reflect on what will matter most at death.*
> *And so resolve to make the most of my life.*

3. actions have consequences

Next comes the reminder that actions have consequences. Everything we do has an effect on the world around us. It also has an effect on the kind of person we become. In Buddhism, these effects are known as *karma-vipaka*. Put simply, this means that we are constantly creating ourselves through what we do, say, or even think. Our individuality is made up of our past choices. If we have spent our lives being generous and open-handed, we become more giving, but in a more spontaneous way. It becomes easier for us, it is natural to the way we are, the whole way we tend to think and feel becomes full of richness and generosity. Conversely, if we've spent years being tight-fisted, this, too, becomes a habit and develops into an innate tendency. We find ourselves becoming meaner and more pinched in our attitude and behaviour towards others.

In this reflection, we try to think back on our lives and see the forces that have conditioned us, but we also see how we have responded to them and created ourselves through these responses. We can think of the influence of our parents, siblings, or the culture in which we grew up, or teachers at school. What choices can we see we have made through our lives and what have been the consequences? Do we have regrets from the past? What about the things we've done well? Particularly in the ethical sphere, can we spot habits in ourselves that we may have been reinforcing for many years?

Again, the purpose of the reflection is not to make us despair, but to give us confidence and hope. The truth of impermanence means that everything changes. If we understand more fully that actions have consequences, we can change our own lives. So, in this reminder, we can recall how we've changed too. We realize how fully and deeply we are responsible for ourselves, and this can be both challenging and liberating. In the reflection below, I've put the emphasis on our positive qualities and the ways we can, and have, changed for the better.

Communication technology today gives us a previously undreamed of access to information and news from all over the world. A potential downside is that we are overwhelmed by a sense of powerlessness. We see so much suffering on our TV screens and wonder what on earth we can do about it. If we are not careful, this can subtly erode our sense that our actions do have consequences. Do you ever feel, 'what difference can I make to problems on such a vast scale? What difference can I make if everyone else is just carrying on oblivious to the issues?' So it is especially important to reflect that all actions have consequences, and to renew in us a sense of the significance of our moral lives. There is a story of a man walking along a beach on which thousands of starfish had been washed up by a storm. He started throwing the starfish back into the water, one by one. Someone came along and asked him why he was bothering. What was the point when there were so many thousands of starfish stranded on the shore? 'Well,' said the man, throwing another starfish back into the ocean, 'it makes a difference to this one … and to this one … and to this one.' Everything we do has an effect, however small, on the world. Every action is also significant in that it affects the kind of person we become.

I am the product of so many complex conditions.
I was born into a particular country and time in history.
I had certain parents and family and upbringing.
All these things will have deeply affected who I am.

But my own actions also condition my future.
And my actions have an effect on the world around me.

Let me recall some of the good I have done.
There are times when I have offered help and friendship.
There are times when I've spoken true and kind words.
There are many times that, even in small ways,
I have made a difference to those around me.

I am responsible for my life and actions.
Let me resolve to act from the good.
Let me try to avoid harming myself and others.
Let me try to be a force for good in the world.

4. suffering

The fourth and final reminder is that there is suffering in life. We try to look honestly at our own lives and to acknowledge or admit those things – large or small – that we find unsatisfactory. They might be physical discomforts or hardships, painful relationships, or dissatisfaction with an aspect of life such as our job. We can try to see that all this is part of life. Everyone experiences dissatisfaction; not just us.

This doesn't imply that we should be passive in relation to difficulties and not try to put them right where possible. It is rather that reflecting in this way can help us relate to our suffering or dissatisfaction more lightly, and avoid unhelpful responses such as self-pity. We can also see that since the world is large and complex and ever changing, we are never going to get things exactly how we want them.

If we watch TV or look in newspapers, we soon become aware of suffering on a larger scale. In the world around us we see conflict, oppression, famine, and natural disasters. Closer to home we see sickness, the indignity of old age, mental illness, depression, anxiety, stress. We see that even people who have so much materially are often unhappy and restless, and can behave in ways that cause themselves more suffering.

Maybe we feel we don't need to be reminded of this. Why would we want to think about such things? Awareness of suffering can be uncomfortable, so sometimes we want to forget it, shut it out, and desensitize ourselves. But this fourth reflection encourages us to be aware of the reality of this side of life. Challenging though it is, it might help us to avoid being complacent about our lives. Like the first reminder, it helps us to see how lucky we are, most of the time. It can also discourage any tendency to think of the Buddhist life being about creating a cosy, peaceful escape from the world, and help us instead to be compassionately aware of the world. It can encourage us to make the most of opportunities to act with kindness and relieve suffering whenever we can.

If, however, we do feel ourselves becoming despondent or overwhelmed, it is good to go back to the first reminder and restore a sense of the preciousness of life.

> *I can't entirely avoid suffering.*
> *There will be times of illness and discomfort.*
> *There will be times when life doesn't give me what I want.*
> *Sometimes people, even trusted friends, will disappoint me.*
> *This is part of life.*

17

It happens to me, and it happens to everyone.
So how should I resolve to respond to suffering in my life?

Life is constant change.
I will never get everything in my life to stay just how I want!
I should resolve to remember this truth.

All around me I see so much suffering.
On TV there are wars, famines, or disasters.
On the streets I see people suffering stress, old age, or lack of meaning.
In nature, many animals are either hunting or being hunted.
There is always a struggle for survival.

Sometimes I can act with kindness and relieve suffering.
Let me resolve to try to do this when I can.
At other times, I cannot take away all the suffering I see.
But at least I can be aware of the pain of others.
I can hold their suffering – tenderly – in my heart.

* * *

When people use these reflections they are often surprised at how stirring they can be, and also how they can feel strangely liberating. They seem to bring us back to that sense of what is essential, who we really are, and what truly matters about our lives.

It is with this sense of the stories of our individual lives, and our desire to discover their deepest possibilities, that the Buddhist life begins. We may feel increasing discontent at splashing around in the shallows, and want to swim into the deep. There is an emerging awareness of old habits of behaviour, patterns of communication, and ways of thinking that hold us back. We want to break out and change direction. But we often need help in knowing how to go about this, and Buddhism offers a wide range of practical methods for bringing about this self-transformation. It is to these tools for living your life that we now turn.

2

mindfulness

knowing yourself

Siddhartha Gautama, the young man who one day became the Buddha, discovered a vital clue about how to pursue his spiritual quest.

He had left the comfort of his home to pursue the spiritual life, and had spent many years making incredible efforts in meditation, striving for Enlightenment with all the willpower he could muster. In the society of that time, some people believed that the way to freedom of the spirit was through denial of the body, so he tried the ascetic path too. He starved himself and tortured his body by meditating for hours in the fierce heat of the sun, but after years of effort it got him nowhere. He realized he was no nearer his goal than the day he had left home. This was a moment of crisis, a low point in his life when a lesser person might have given up in despair. But at precisely this moment a childhood memory returned to him. He intuitively knew this incident contained a vital clue to his search.

He remembered a spring day in his childhood when he had been taken out to see the fields being ploughed for the new season. He was sitting under a rose-apple tree, which was full of delicate, pale blossom. The sun shone and sparkled through the leaves of the trees. It was a lovely scene, full of hope for the coming year, and all this beauty delighted the little boy and transported him, quite naturally and spontaneously, into a meditative state.

Up until that time in his search, he had been striving in meditation with all his mental might. He had been willing his mind into higher states of consciousness. These experiences were supremely blissful while they lasted, but once he 'came down' from his meditation, the young man found he was just the same as before.

But on that day, under the rose-apple tree, he'd tasted a different kind of meditative state, one that was unforced and natural. Rather than wilfully narrowing his mind, he'd experienced a consciousness that was alive and open, as well as calm and concentrated. The result was a mind that was tranquil, steady, and serene.

The traditional legends of the Buddha's life now go on to tell how, with this new understanding of how to meditate, he sat in a beautiful spot under the shade of a tree, and gained Enlightenment that very night. But maybe it was not quite like that. Perhaps the young man did have a new understanding, but also had to develop and refine it. He made use of old techniques of meditation, but adapted them. He evolved his own way of delving into the depths of the mind and revealing its potential. Over the weeks and months he steadily meditated, gradually transforming the contents of his mind, until one night he did finally realize that he had found his goal and that his task was complete.[5]

The path of meditation that the Buddha discovered was the way of mindfulness. Mindfulness is a way of being in which we pay careful attention to all our experience. This includes our inner thoughts and feelings, as well as our outer experience – the sensations and impressions that come to us through the senses. Whatever we experience we try to imbue with this kind and receptive awareness, but without craving positive experiences or encouraging negative thoughts and emotions. When we do this we become more rooted, more connected with our inner life. Our habits and tendencies become more apparent, and this puts us in a position from which we can begin to change them.

This teaching and practice of mindfulness is central to Buddhism. In the traditional accounts of the Buddha's life, we see him time and again teaching his followers how to develop mindfulness and exhorting them to maintain it at all times. His very last words were, 'With mindfulness, strive on.'

For many people, their first encounter with Buddhism is this teaching about mindfulness, and some of the meditation techniques that can help us to develop it. This is a good and obvious place to begin. Without mindfulness, and an understanding of what is going on within our hearts and minds, we cannot really begin to change ourselves and our situation. Mindfulness is the starting point: the opening up of possibility.

The practice of mindfulness was a revelation to me. Although I had studied psychology at university for three years, no one had ever suggested that I could watch my heart and mind in this way, and that I could actually learn about my inner self and then be able to change. In this chapter we will first explore how we can cultivate mindfulness in meditation, and then look at the practice of mindfulness in daily life.

mindfulness meditation

Meditation involves, above all, becoming more aware of our hearts and minds. One meditation practice designed to help us cultivate mindfulness is called the mindfulness of breathing.[6] In this practice we sit quietly and 'watch' the breath. We follow the bodily sensations caused by the flow of the breath.

exercise – *following the breath*

For now, we are going to try the breathing meditation in a very simple way. Full instructions for meditation practices are not given in this book. There are books that do this, but it is better to attend a meditation class and receive direction from an experienced teacher.

Sitting quietly and comfortably (on a meditation cushion if you know how to sit comfortably, or otherwise on a chair), relax your body for a few minutes, while remaining awake and aware. You might find it best to close your eyes gently, or you may keep them softly open.

> *Then start noticing how your body breathes. Don't try to breathe in any special way, just breathe naturally. Feel the sensations of the breath in different parts of the body. Where do you feel the breath? What is the in-breath like? And what about the out-breath?*
>
> *Try to stay focused on the breath. If you notice your mind wandering, just bring it back to attending to the breath. If your mind starts to wander, try to notice this immediately. Do this for up to ten minutes.*
>
> *Afterwards, consider what happened. Was it easy to stay alert and focused, or was it difficult? Were you surprised at the kind of things that went through your mind?*

This is how we can begin in meditation, and from that simple starting point, our practice develops further. I'll tell you a little of how it worked for me. When I first took up meditation, I did it in rather a mechanical way, watching the breath on one spot of my body, counting the breaths robotically, and trying all the time not to let anything else enter my mind. Although it was too mechanical, at least it got me started. If the teacher had said straight off, 'be aware of your mind,' I wouldn't have known what he meant, or where to start. The first thing I needed to do was just learn to be able to sit and be focused. But after a while, I realized there was more to the practice than rigidly following the breath. Tuning in to the breath enabled my mind to slow a little. There was now enough space for a broader view; I could see more clearly what was going on in my mind and heart. I realized that those thoughts and feelings I was trying to shut out were actually part of me. They were aspects of the mind I was trying to transform. I could not transform them until I let them in, acknowledged them, and came to know them more deeply.

We have to learn to work in a multi-layered kind of way. With some types of distracting thoughts or worries, it might be enough to put them aside and return to the breath. If there is not much energy behind them, this might be sufficient to transform them. But, in other cases, that could take longer. We might find various ways of working with the breath that help, for example breathing low in the body if we are anxious, or breathing more slowly if we are angry. We sit with the worry or irritation *at the same time* as we sit with the breath. With this 'mindfulness *with* breathing' we explore the connection between the quality of the breath and our mental and emotional state.[7] At other times, we might need to just sit with what is happening in our heart and mind, without attending to the breath at all. Perhaps there is something that nags at us and we need to uncover it, try to reveal its nature. Perhaps we need to reflect on why we have got irritated yet again, or why it is that a certain situation makes us anxious. So, for a while at least, we leave the breath and just attend to the issue at hand. But we have made a conscious decision to do this. We haven't stopped cultivating mindfulness, only adopted a different approach for the time being. Mindfulness meditation is not just a rigid technique; it is a way of being with our actual experience, attuned to our hearts and minds, and being able to respond helpfully to what we find there. Our approach needs to be subtle, nuanced according to the strength and nature of what is happening right now. The crucial factor is that we are trying to become more aware, and notice what is happening in our minds, without letting it run away with us.

There is another meditation method that can be helpful in learning this ability to sit in awareness.

exercise – *just sitting*

In this exercise we sit quietly and comfortably as in the first meditation, but this time we are not going to focus on anything in particular.

We just watch the play of our minds. We try to notice any thoughts, sensations, or feelings as they come into the mind. If we have a thought about a meeting we have to attend tomorrow, we simply watch the thought as it comes and goes. If there is an itch in our left leg, we feel the itch and it fades away. If we hear a neighbour shouting, we simply hear the sound come and go. If we notice irritation arising, we feel the irritation and let it go.

We try this for maybe five minutes and then relax for a few moments. Afterwards we can reflect on what happened. Was it easy, or was it difficult? Were we surprised by the activity of the mind?

Sitting in this way, you might notice how your mind has an inexhaustible tendency to reach out, and either want to grasp or to repel the experiences it finds out there. But in this exercise we are attempting to rest the mind in simple mindfulness: relaxing, rather than grasping or repelling. This type of meditation is sometimes called the just sitting practice, but we need to be careful that we are not just drifting! We do not want to lose ourselves in the play of the mind, but remain fully aware. This is not always easy and may require a lot of practice.

Through meditation, we come to know our minds more fully, and we might be surprised by what we discover. Sometimes the sheer volume of thoughts rushing round in our head is shocking. We may discover anger and irritation that has not been fully acknowledged, emotions that have been gnawing away at our hearts without our realizing. There are happier discoveries too; we free up more expansive emotion and energy, and may experience new levels of clarity and calm. We can gradually come to learn about the deeper and subtler workings of the mind, and there is always more to discover.

Cultivating this mindfulness also gives us distance from which we can see the overall pattern of our lives. It allows us to untangle ourselves from the daily worries, irritations, and concerns and create a space around them. In this space we can know ourselves more clearly and see what is really going on and what is truly important to us. Our habits and tendencies become more apparent. If they are unhelpful habits this means we can now change them. So mindfulness is the first crucial step to our inner freedom, to becoming more fully the 'author' of our own story.

But cultivating mindfulness also takes time. Sometimes, when teaching meditation, I've asked people why they want to learn. A common reply is, 'I just want to be able to switch off.' I have to disappoint them. Our minds are not computers. We cannot just click on an icon, or flick a switch, to quell the activity of the mind. In the previous chapter we saw how what we are is the product of all our previous thoughts, words, and acts. This is true on many levels: on the macro- level, when we look back at our whole life and see the kind of person we have become, but also on a micro-, or day-to-day, level. The thoughts and images that may be swirling round our heads right now are the product of what we've been thinking, saying, and doing this very day. There is no magical technique to just stop all this; we have to sit with the mind, letting that *karma-vipaka* (see p.14) gradually play itself out.

There is a lovely traditional image for this. Imagine your mind is like a glass vessel of water. Perhaps the water is muddy and unclear, with various bits and pieces swimming about in it. Meditation is sitting quietly and still so that the sediment gradually starts to settle. It takes time, but after a while the water becomes crystal clear and still. This process cannot be hurried. Anything you do to the water to try to *make* it clear will actually stir it up again.

Since meditation works gradually, consistency of practice over time is also very important. Meditating every day for a short period, or at least most days in a week, is much better that a long meditation only once or twice a week. You can also experiment to see what works best for you: meditating first thing in the day, or at another time? Is meditating for about twenty minutes right for you, or could you usefully go a bit longer?

exercise – *daily meditation practice*

You might find the following helpful in encouraging you to establish a daily meditation. Try to meditate once a day, or as many days as you can manage, for the next two weeks. It doesn't have to be a long meditation. If you miss a day, don't give up, but get back to it as soon as you can. It is often recommended that we alternate the mindfulness of breathing that we explored above with the loving-kindness meditation described in the next chapter. But for now, if you've only learned one meditation, just do that one every day.

Perhaps you could even keep a meditation journal for these two weeks, briefly recording at the end of each session what happened, and anything you learned or noticed that you want to remember and take forward to the next meditation.

After two weeks, ask whether you notice any difference in yourself. You might be surprised at what you find. You could even ask your friends if they notice any difference. Other people sometimes notice more quickly than we do!

Daily practice allows the meditation to have a cumulative effect. Establishing a daily practice is a significant stage in making meditation a central part of our lives. We try to develop a positive habit in which we meditate every day when our practice is going well, but also keeping going when it seems harder.

mindfulness in daily life

When we start to notice how our meditation is affected by the thoughts and concerns of our everyday activity, we are led to an important realization. Mindfulness is a quality that we need to practise all the time, from moment to moment.

There is a two-way relationship at work here. First, the mindfulness we cultivate in our meditation will permeate our daily lives. After we've been meditating for a while we may well notice that we are a bit calmer and more aware as we go about our everyday business. The spaciousness of meditation flavours the rest of our experience.

Secondly, the mindfulness we cultivate from day to day makes our meditation practice more fruitful. If mindfulness is about knowing ourselves better, then we need to attend to what happens in every moment. In meditation we can watch the mind directly, but there is just as much to be learned about ourselves through our daily experience. The way to see ourselves really clearly is often through our interactions with others. Away from it all, in the quiet of our meditation, it might be easy to kid ourselves, but in the thick of daily life, with demands and pressures on us, we can see what our real strengths and weaknesses are. This creates the raw material for our meditation.

exercise – *mindfulness moments*

> *Practising mindfulness in everyday life is not easy – there can be so much information to process, so much to distract us. But there are techniques we can use to help us.*[8]
>
> *For example, we may use something as a cue to re-establish mindfulness. Every time the phone rings, or each time we make a cup of tea, we try to remember to come back to ourselves. We can just stop and breathe deeply a few times, and then continue with what we were doing, but with renewed attentiveness and presence.*
>
> *Or we might make sure there are at least a few short, but empty, spaces in our day when we can recollect ourselves.*
>
> *Choose one such method and try it for a week. What do you notice about your quality of mind in those spaces of awareness? Does the effect of 'mindfulness moments' spill out into the rest of your day? Do you find it easy to remember to be mindful, or difficult?*

bare awareness and continuity of purpose

In order to explore further how we might develop mindfulness in daily life, we're going to look in a little more detail at two dimensions of awareness drawn out in the texts from the early Buddhist tradition.[9] First, *sati*, a Pali word which could be translated as 'bare awareness'. Secondly, *sampajanna*, or 'continuity of purpose'.

Bare awareness is that simple state of being collected, rather then semi-absent. You are more fully present in your experience. Your body, senses, heart, and mind are alive and receptive. You feel as though your feet are firmly on the ground – earthed and connected.

Some people can remember a moment in their childhood when they first became self-aware. I can remember one very ordinary day when I was about 4 or 5 years old. I was in the bathroom washing my hands and I can clearly recall the sandy orange of the walls, the white ceramic sink gleaming under the electric light, turning the soap in my hands, and holding my hands under the running water. Suddenly, there was this strange sense of excitement and wonder that this was happening to *me* right now, right there. Perhaps bare awareness has something of the freshness and immediacy of that experience. We are aware, and aware of being aware. Perhaps you can recall other times or places in your life when your awareness has felt heightened in this way.

When we dwell in this kind of bare awareness, we become more attuned to things. Our awareness becomes more refined, subtle, and sensitive. We notice small changes and more detail. We look more, so we see more. Only those who know how to 'stop and stare' will notice the primroses nestling in the hedgerow, catch sight of a sparrowhawk as it hurtles through the trees, or enjoy the sodium orange of the street lamp splashing and sparkling on wet tarmac on a winter's night.

Part of what we are doing in the mindfulness of breathing meditation is cultivating this ability to be attuned. Do you find that the more you watch the breath, the more you notice? Do you begin to feel fine and subtle sensations where you have not noticed them before? Perhaps we start to realize that we breathe with our whole bodies, not just our lungs. We might pay attention to how there are four stages to each breath: the in-breath and the out-breath, but there is also a pause between in and out, and also between out and in. Can you watch and feel the similarities and differences in the duration, texture, and depth of each of these phases of the breath? Even something as ordinary as the breath can become rich and pleasurable.

Having this quality to our experience doesn't entail having to do everything incredibly slowly. A pianist playing a fast and difficult piece of music may pour his or her fingers over the keyboard very, very quickly, while still being completely concentrated and absorbed such that they are one with the music. Sometimes doing an activity physically slowly *can* help slow down the mind and establish *sati*, but it doesn't always follow that acting slowly equals mindfulness, or acting quickly equals mindlessness. It is the quality of awareness that counts, not the speed.

The second aspect of mindfulness is continuity of purpose. Mindfulness is not only about being attuned to the present moment, but also about how what happens now will affect and condition what happens in the future. We try to remain aware of our purpose, where it is that we want to go. When we establish this quality, our lives becomes more whole and harmonious. We don't distractedly drop one activity because we suddenly realize we need to get on with the next, but there is a flow from one activity to another. Ideally, we retain a sense of continuity and harmony in which every aspect of our lives is related to all the others.

Here is an example of this continuity of purpose in action. Let's say that at your workplace you are responsible for the maintenance of the buildings. You've recently noticed in your meditation a growing anxiety centred on your job. Your purpose is to become less anxious, so you remember this in your meditation over the next few days. You keep coming back to that anxiety and, using the breath, try to work with it appropriately. Not only that, you retain this sense of purpose at work. You start examining when and why you get anxious. Perhaps you notice that the anxiety arises when you leave things to the last moment, so you try to become more organized. And then you extend your continuity of purpose even further. Over the next few weeks you reflect more deeply on the anxious patterns, and perhaps discover an underlying view that is unhelpful and contributing to the anxiety. This semi-conscious belief is that you should be able to get things done and finished. You realize you are always racing to bring things to a complete and perfect state by the end of the week, but you now see that, in reality, there is no such thing as finished. With the maintenance of a large old building there will always be another job to do. So you take this little insight back into your meditation and try to loosen up, and relax unhelpful attitudes and expectations. Then you try to apply this quality of looseness back at work, and see if there are further changes to be made to the way you function. In this way, you are all the time retaining your sense of purpose, exploring your life more and more deeply, bringing it back to meditation and bringing meditation into your life.

This quality of mindfulness isn't about being delicate. Builders can be just as mindful as ballet dancers. In fact, mindfulness makes us more robust and steady. In the traditional stories about the Buddha, he is often described as being like an elephant. At that time, elephants would have been associated with royalty, but we can see that comparing the Buddha to an elephant might also have been a way of describing his mindfulness. Elephants are big, but they are not clumsy. In fact, they move in a very solid, definite, and also graceful kind of way. Apparently, elephants also look at things with a very steady gaze, and when they turn to look, they turn their whole bodies. I imagine that if an elephant was looking at us, we would feel we were receiving very full attention.

Mindfulness does also have a simple beauty to it. When I was a teenager, my family went on holiday to Guernsey, where we stayed with an old friend of my mother. Boop, as she was known, was not a Buddhist, but she had practised meditation and yoga for many years. I can remember thinking there was something different about her, but I didn't know what it was. I would now say that she had a depth of mindfulness such as I'd not encountered before: her brown eyes were clear and sparkling, her face was open and expressive, and she moved with elegance and poise. Above all, she seemed self-aware and understanding of others. This impressed me deeply and, probably without her ever knowing it, she was a significant influence on my life.

3

loving-kindness
learning to love

In the previous chapter we explored how the cultivation of mindfulness leads to greater self-awareness. In this chapter we will be looking at how to become more aware of others.

Although we may aspire to being more kind, or patient, or calm, the heart doesn't always respond the way our head thinks it should. We need other ways of connecting to a heart that is more open and at ease, more able to love.

Loving-kindness can be defined as a warm, concerned, awareness of ourselves and other people. When we love, we want others to be happy and to have what they need to be truly happy. This sounds very nice in theory, but a difficulty arises when another person's needs or wants do not coincide with our own. It is in these situations that our relationships with people are really tested. Loving does not entail ignoring our own needs, but neither does it mean always putting our needs above those of everyone else. Sometimes you meet people who behave in one or other of these extreme ways. The martyr constantly sacrifices himself or herself, but deep down is full of resentment, while the immaturely selfish person goes about life completely oblivious of other people. The art of loving lies in nurturing awareness of both our own and others' needs, negotiating between them appropriately and with kindness and generosity of spirit.

There is a meditation practice designed to help develop this loving heart, known traditionally as the *metta bhavana*. These are two Pali words, the first of which is usually translated 'loving-kindness', the second as 'cultivation' or 'development'. So in this chapter we are going to be exploring the cultivation of loving-kindness. We will consider how we can develop love and positive emotion by looking at how this particular meditation practice works.

The meditation is performed in five stages. While sitting quietly, you cultivate this well-wishing attitude first towards yourself, then towards a good friend, then a 'neutral' person (someone you don't know well, or don't strongly like or dislike), then towards someone you find difficult, and then to as many living beings as possible – gradually expanding out and including more and more. So we can see that the loving-kindness meditation is structured in a way that reflects the need to be aware of self as well as of others.

When we first take up this practice, we might do it very simply. For example, as you choose a person to bring to mind in each of the five stages, you just quietly say certain words or phrases to yourself, such as 'May I/they be well,' 'may I/they be happy,' 'may I/they be free from suffering,' 'may I/they fulfil my/their highest potential.' Just dropping these phrases into your heart can be like dropping pebbles into a deep pool – a ripple expands outwards. It may be surprising that something so simple can work, but currents of more positive emotion can indeed be coaxed into being, or positive emotion that is already present can be given more momentum and strength.

However, as we saw in the previous chapter when we explored the mindfulness of breathing, meditation involves more than mechanically counting breaths or reciting phrases. As we gain experience in the practice, we learn to take a broader, more varied approach. It is good to experiment and use our imagination – any method that helps us be more emotionally aware and develop loving-kindness is valid. So we will now look at the meditation stage by stage and examine some possible techniques.

ourselves

People are sometimes surprised that a meditation in which we are learning to love should start with ourselves. But the practice is just acknowledging the psychological truth that we cannot go out to others in an emotionally positive way unless we have positive emotion for ourselves. We first need a sense of our own self-worth and an appreciation of life and its potential. In our culture this seems difficult for some people. An unforgiving self-criticism, or subtle, underlying sense of worthlessness, is surprisingly common.

Most of us talk to ourselves; there is an internal voice providing us with a running commentary on our day. What is the emotional tone of this voice? Are we talking to ourselves in a way in which we wouldn't dare talk to others? Is the voice harsh, moaning, or over-critical? If so, can we soften the voice, and let it be kinder and more forgiving?

Or is it a voice of self-pity, feeling let down by other people and blaming the world for our misery? Such self-pity is corrosive. Even if we *have* been let down by others, it is no use wallowing in these feelings. Eventually we need to pick ourselves up, dust ourselves down, and start again. In order to be able to do this, we need to acknowledge our pain, admit to ourselves that we were hurt, and bring to this hurt a sense of kindness.

Perhaps our inner voice isn't usually so negative, but we notice that it can become so in certain situations. When things don't go our way, this might trigger a particular way in which we speak to ourselves. It might be worth exploring all this in meditation and in daily life.

This first stage of the meditation may also help us find the emotional resources to deal with stress and difficulty in our lives. If life is currently hard or painful, we can practise 'self-empathy'. We take the time to listen to ourselves, to hear about what is difficult, with kindness and understanding. We do the same with ourselves as we would with a friend who was suffering – we try just to listen with empathy.

I've recently taught this practice to groups of carers – people who are caring long-term for a severely ill or disabled family member. They are ordinary people from whom so much energy and self-sacrifice is required on an ongoing basis. They relate very easily to this need for self-empathy, for the time to look at their own emotional resources, in order to be able to go on coping with the daily demands of caring. Sometimes they have to deal with feelings of guilt. If the pressures on them are great, they can understandably start to feel anger towards the person for whom they are caring. On top of this, they feel guilty about feeling anger. Self-empathy can help bring to this a kindness and understanding of one's humanity and limitations. At other times they can feel equally uneasy about feeling good – why should they feel happy when their near and dear one is in pain? Self-empathy can help them realize that they are human beings that deserve happiness too. Also, if they are able to feel more emotionally buoyant and resilient, this is not selfish because it means they will have the emotional resources carry on helping others.

As well as working with negative feelings towards ourselves, we can also remind ourselves of our positive qualities. We can look at our lives and see that we do act with loving-kindness much of the time, even if it is sometimes mixed with other motives, or even if we don't always feel hugely positive. But we can give ourselves credit for what is positive.

Extending on from this, we can also use this stage of the practice to strengthen positive qualities, or to develop new ones. I often work by imagining qualities that I would like to develop. I try to envisage what it would be like to have those qualities. For example, if I've noticed myself getting irritated in meetings at work, I imagine how it might be possible to make my points in the meeting without the irritation, and with more kindness to others. I sit trying to be open to the possibility. Sometimes this imaginative approach helps me see my potential more clearly. I can sense quite tangibly how I *could* be different. Then I actually start to *feel* different.

We might also spend time reflecting on all that is good in our lives, cultivating a sense of gratitude and appreciation (a bit like the reminder of the preciousness of life in Chapter 1). By doing this, we can gain a different perspective on the things we tend to moan about – we realize that they are not that bad. We can feel richer, more expansive, and warmed up – ready for the subsequent stages of the practice.

exercise – *imagining new possibilities*

You can try the various ideas and approaches suggested above in your meditation practice. It would probably be best to spread them out over a few weeks, rather than trying them all at once. You could take notes as you go, and see if there are some you find more helpful than others.

If you already do the loving-kindness practice, you can incorporate them into that. If not, you could start by spending five minutes on one of the approaches suggested above. For example, after relaxing the body and watching the breath for a while, you could try imagining new possibilities. Bring to mind particular, specific, situations in which you have a desire to be different, and recall what you are like in them, how you actually feel in your heart, mind, and body. Allow a sense of how you could be different to emerge, of how you could approach those situations in a new way.

a good friend

In the second stage of the loving-kindness meditation, we bring to mind a good friend, someone towards whom it will be relatively easy for us to feel warm and appreciative. In this phase of the practice, we can work to see them more deeply, see what their qualities are – their own, unique sparkle that makes them the person they are. Maybe we can imagine this sparkle, this quality, shining in them more and more brightly. This is what we desire – for them to be at their very best and happiest.

If our friend is currently happy and healthy and life is going well for them, we bring their good fortune and good qualities to mind and try to respond with a sense of gladness and celebration. On the other hand, if we know they are experiencing difficulties and unhappiness, we can bring that to mind, be as fully aware of them and their situation as we can. We can then try to cultivate a response of empathy and well-wishing.

When this practice is taught to people for the first time, it is often recommended that we do not put someone to whom we are sexually attracted in this stage of the practice. It is also recommended not to include someone who has died, or who is a lot older or younger than us. This is so that our feelings of loving-kindness can be developed without confusion with feelings of a sexual or romantic attraction, grief or remorse, or parental or filial feelings. It is not that there is anything wrong with such feelings, but that we are trying to cultivate loving-kindness to someone with whom our relationship is relatively straightforward, so that we can get a clear idea of what the practice entails.

However, it is also important to emphasize that this is only the case when you are new to the practice. Once you have got an idea of how it works, it is good to include all sorts of people. Indeed, we want to be able to respond with loving-kindness to everyone and anyone, including those we are close to and with whom we are enjoying an intimate relationship. People can sometimes get into the habit of not including certain people, and go on not including them when it would be very appropriate to do so.

exercise – *celebrating friends*
You could start off this phase of the practice with an emphasis on celebrating and appreciating your friend's good qualities. It might seem obvious what their strengths are, and what you value about them, so that thinking about it doesn't seem necessary. However, if you allow time for reflection, a deeper appreciation can emerge. You can start to discern what combination of qualities it is that is uniquely theirs. In other words, they become more special, more loved for who they really are.

You can do this by bearing a friend in mind, or seeing them in your mind's eye. Think of them at different times and in different situations, and with different people. What are they really like?

Do they have distinctive qualities you've not fully noticed before? Are there aspects of them, or memories of times spent with them, that you have not thought about for a long time? We can bring all this to mind and allow appreciation to emerge.

a neutral person

In the third stage we think of a neutral person. Here the practice is presenting us with a particular challenge, that of overcoming indifference. We are being asked to be concerned for someone in whom we have no personal investment. In the second stage we like the person, enjoy their company, and want their friendship. In the fourth stage we are going to be thinking of a difficult person, someone whose company we would rather be without. In each case, a different 'vested interest' is at stake. But the neutral person is in-between. We have no particular feelings, or interests, either way.

The neutral person might be someone we see quite often, but we have no real connection with. It might be a man at work whose name we know, but who we've never really spoken to, or a woman who runs the local corner shop. So in this stage of the practice we are trying to develop a well-wishing towards such a person. Even though we don't know them personally, and may never know them, we want our attitude to be one of desiring their happiness.

Sometimes we can find this stage difficult precisely because we don't have a connection with that person. How can we think about someone if we don't know anything about them? We can try using our imagination. Although we might not know very much about this person's life, we can imagine what it might be like. We can do this is a way which seems realistic, a view of what life might possibly entail for them. What would it be like to work in that shop all day long? You hope she enjoys her work, and that the business is doing well. You imagine where she grew up, what her life might have been like. Though she might be neutral to us, to some other people she is far from that. Perhaps she has a family, and we can hope that they, too, are happy and well. When we are in a hurry, people like her can seem to be two-dimensional figures. They are always there behind the counter when we nip in for our pint of milk or bar of chocolate. In this stage of the practice we are trying to see them more as alive, three-dimensional, human beings. We start to see that we are connected to them more than we think. It is only because she works all those hours that we can call in just when we want to.

exercise – *putting ourselves in their shoes*

If you are not already doing the full loving-kindness practice, you can now try incorporating this third stage into your meditation. Start building up the practice stage by stage. Spend a few minutes on stages one and two every day, and then move on to stage three.

You can do this by bringing to mind someone you see at work, in a shop, or on the bus. Try to imagine being in their shoes. What would it be like to live that life? Fill out as much detail as you can, but obviously there will be aspects of their life you cannot know about. At these times, you can just dwell on the 'mystery' of the other person.

It is good to choose one person and keep them in your practice for a week, or even longer. Then you might want to choose someone else for a while.

You can also do this reflection while you are sitting on the bus, or walking down the street, just looking about you and having a sense of curiosity and kindness towards the people you see about you.

A friend of mine once told me the following story. He used to work in a restaurant where there was a man who came in for lunch every day. He was quiet and never said very much, and the staff in the restaurant used to refer to him as Mr Customer. One day my friend started putting Mr Customer in his neutral-person stage. A few days later, when serving this man, without any particular intention, he started chatting to him. (Let us hope he didn't call him Mr Customer to his face!) This story shows the effect the practice can have. My friend naturally and spontaneously started seeing that man differently. We encounter scores of neutral people every day, and it is worth remembering that, before we knew them, our dearest friends were, to us, just neutral people.

People sometimes make astonishing sacrifices for total strangers. There are many stories of people giving their lives trying to save others in a disaster or emergency – rushing back into a burning building, or diving into freezing cold water. They are only 'ordinary' people, but such stories provide food for thought about our potential for self-transcendence and concern for others. Perhaps you could even say there is only such a thing as 'society' to the extent that we can identify with 'neutral' people. If we didn't have any concern for neutral people, society would soon break down.

the person we find difficult

In the fourth stage of the practice, we become aware of someone we find difficult, irritating, or antagonistic. We try to overcome any ill will and, instead, cultivate a concern for their welfare. This is very challenging indeed and we may feel a resistance even to the idea of attempting it! But, although it seems counter-intuitive, the best chance for our own happiness consists in thinking about the happiness of others.

When we are new to the practice, it might be best to start with someone we experience as just mildly awkward or irritating, rather than someone we find really difficult. Otherwise we may end our lovingkindness meditation with gritted teeth and steam coming out of our ears! With time and experience, we learn how to work in this stage of the practice and may feel robust enough to take on those whom we find more seriously difficult. I know many people who have gradually transformed deep negative feelings towards certain people, or vastly improved key relationships in their life that have been problematic.

In this stage of the practice we first simply acknowledge our feelings, owning any anger or ill will, and just trying to soften, relax, and let it go. We can reflect on how useless such feelings are. They just cause pain and disturbance in our minds and, if we act from that basis, they also cause pain for others.

When we are in a state of hatred, we don't see the other person as they really are. We see what we dislike writ large, so that we can't appreciate other aspects of them. In the meditation we can work against this tendency, bringing to mind their positive qualities, and reflecting that although we don't like them, there are probably other people who do. Our view of them is only part of the story.

It is worth being aware of assumptions. Someone we don't like arrives late for a meeting and we complain to ourselves. 'She is always late. She's just avoiding this meeting because she knows its not going to go her way.' Then she turns up, full of apologies, and explains that on the way to work she found a little boy who'd lost his mother, so she had to help him. We sit there feeling glad we'd not criticized her out loud! Perhaps our policy should be to give people the benefit of the doubt, trying to assume the best about them and their motives. Maybe we need to be especially careful with those we find difficult, when we can often be overly suspicious of their motives. Of course, this does not mean being naive. If we know full well they are taking us for a ride, we need to do something about it. But we should be careful that we do know for sure, rather than jumping to a conclusion.

As well as trying to loosen *our* narrow, subjective view of the person we find difficult, we can go even further and attempt to look at the situation from *their* point of view. For example, I'm irritated because someone is being a bit antagonistic towards me at work. He makes the odd sarcastic comment and seems opposed to anything I suggest. Perhaps in the meditation I can reflect on why he might be doing this. There *will* be a reason. He did it because, rightly or wrongly, consciously or unconsciously, he thought it would make him happy. He, like everyone else, and like me, just wants to be happy, so he acts in ways that he thinks will produce this happiness. But how was it that he thought being sarcastic could contribute to his happiness? Perhaps I was a bit short with him the previous day and, feeling hurt, he is trying to show me his determination not to be treated like that. Realizing this, I can try to take his point of view into account. I can try to speak to him more sensitively.

Or perhaps I recently got promoted to a post that he'd also applied for, and I realize he is feeling rather competitive at the moment. In this case, although his feelings are not my fault, I can still be aware of what is going on and act appropriately. Perhaps I am careful to be extra appreciative of him in the next few weeks (without making it too obvious, of course). Rather than acting on the basis of my irritation, I have looked deeply and seen the situation from the other person's perspective. I can try to act in a way that helps him and, in fact, this will be what helps me too. I'm responding with compassion to his mistaken idea of what will make him happy. Such a compassionate response is more likely to help him towards a better idea of where happiness is to be found.

exercise – *understanding the difficulties of others*

Now you can try incorporating this fourth stage of the meditation into your own practice. Allow a few minutes for each stage until you arrive at the 'difficult person' stage.

You bring this person to mind as in the other stages, and notice and acknowledge your feelings towards them. Then choose one of the approaches explored above.

If your feelings are strong, it might be best just to work on letting go. When you notice your mind following an irritable train of thought, notice the thoughts and then let them go. When you notice anger in your heart, or a physical sense of tightness and tension, try to soften and let go. You can ask yourself if these negative feelings are worth holding on to, and who benefits from them.

Or you can spend time thinking about this person's positive qualities that you do not usually notice or give them credit for. Or you might try to understand why it is they behave in a way you find difficult, try to see the situation from their point of view.

41

Again, it is good to vary the approach over time, to take notes, and notice what works for you.

Sometimes, if your feelings are strong, you cannot deal with them in one meditation. Don't worry about this. If the negative feelings persist, leave that person for a while and come back to stage one of the practice, or just to physical relaxation of the body, or watching the breath.

This is, of course, much harder in practice than in theory. In real life, events unfold so quickly. Our feelings of hurt smart and burn, they seem instantly to transform themselves into indignation or irritation, and then we can't seem to stop ourselves acting on them. But that is why loving-kindness is something we have to practise both within meditation and without. We gradually learn to see things from a more objective, compassionate point of view.

Another aspect of loving-kindness, and of seeing people in a more rounded, realistic way, is forgiveness. My Buddhist teacher once said, 'I am much worse than you think I am, but also much better.'[10] He was asking his followers, who perhaps had a tendency to put him on a pedestal, to try to see him more as he really was – as a person with a mix of good qualities and human weaknesses. The aphorism is true of us all. We are probably all capable of acting in far worse ways than we'd like to think, but we are also capable of much more good than we dare imagine. Human life is complex, and we can only learn as we go along, by making mistakes. When I look back on my life and see the times when I've caused most harm to others, it was not out of a deliberate wish to do so, but out of an insensitivity born of inexperience, or sheer naivety, or because I was blind to the needs of others because of my own desires. Because we will all make mistakes, we need to be able to forgive. We need self-forgiveness and forgiveness towards others. As William Blake said, 'Mutual forgiveness of each vice, such are the Gates of Paradise.'[11]

When someone has done us a serious wrong, forgiveness can be very difficult and may take a long time. However, the example of South Africa is inspiring. When apartheid came to an end, and they had their first democratic elections, there was much debate about how to bring to justice those who had committed atrocities. People eventually realized that retribution through the courts was not an option. Apart from the practical difficulties of providing evidence, there was fear that the whole process would lead to more bitterness and violence. For this reason, some people called for a general amnesty and writing off of crimes. Others argued that this would be to ignore the principle of justice. So a Truth and Reconciliation Committee was formed. Perpetrators were offered amnesty, but only if they came forward and admitted their crimes. Victims were also encouraged to tell of the terrible atrocities that had been inflicted on them or their families. The committee ensured that these stories were heard, including by those who probably committed the crimes. The victims would not have to live with those experiences for the rest of their days without their being acknowledged, or with the rest of the country in denial. And forgiveness – restorative justice rather than retributive justice – was encouraged. There are stories of remarkably courageous acts of forgiveness from many people – both black and white.

Having difficulties with people is, of course, inevitable. We are all so different, and human communication and interaction is bound to be complex and problematic at times. So perhaps it is helpful to realize that difficulties are normal; it is how we deal with them that matters. We cannot expect to get on with everybody all the time, but we can try to bring awareness, understanding, and honesty to the problems that crop up.

expanding outwards

The final stage of the loving-kindness meditation has two aspects. First, we think of the four people in the practice so far (ourselves, the good friend, the neutral person, and the difficult person), and try to cultivate this sense of well-wishing to them equally. Then we gradually include more and more people. We can do this in a number of ways. We could try to sense loving-kindness radiating out in all directions, or even visualize it in the form of light or a colour expanding outwards. Or we might imagine people in different parts of the world.

In our imaginations we can travel north, south, east, and west, trying to get a sense of all the people we might meet. Or we can bring to mind people in different situations. At this very moment babies are being born and old people are breathing their last few breaths, some people are going to bed and others are getting up to a new day, some are facing terrible suffering, while others experience joy.

Sometimes we find this stage of the practice difficult. It may have been going along quite well, but then trying to hold all these people and situations in our imagination is too much and we lose the thread. If this happens, we can take a more modest approach: just thinking of a few people and situations. The principle is simply to expand outwards in whatever way we can.

Whatever technique we use, we are trying to bring about a warm well-wishing to all that live. We want anyone and everyone to be happy. This is a high ideal, but sometimes when this stage of the practice goes well, it feels as though loving-kindness is flowing through us. We can feel light, expansive, and open-hearted.

exercise – *reaching out into the world*

Now incorporate this final stage into your loving-kindness meditation.

You could start by thinking of people in a distant place you have recently seen on TV or read about in a newspaper, putting your-self in their shoes in the same way as in stage three. Or, if this does not help you to connect emotionally, you could try thinking of a distant place you have visited, and the people who are there right now. Alternatively, you might imagine a part of the world where you have a relative or a friend, and then imagine other people around them. The trick is to find some way of establish-ing an emotional connection, but not being impatient if it doesn't always work, or takes a long time.

* * *

Through this meditation, and through using the same principles in our actual daily life, we can radically transform our emotional attitudes. We can come to a much better understanding of our own emotions and learn to see others more kindly.

Of course, we will never completely understand other people and should be careful of being too keen to analyse and think we understand them. Each of our histories, influences, and hidden potentials are too deep and subtle for that. We should always hold our opinions about people with a degree of tentativeness. In fact, we will never completely understand ourselves, let alone other people. As we grow older, one of the things we realize is that we will always be, to some extent, a mystery, even to ourselves. There will be parts of ourselves we never fully perceive or comprehend. Despite this, our understanding of ourselves and of others can always go deeper, and so, in consequence, can our ability to love.

4

ethics

taking practice into the world

Do not take lightly small misdeeds,
Believing they can do no harm:
Even a tiny spark of fire
Can set alight a mountain of hay.

Do not take lightly small good deeds,
Believing they can hardly help:
For drops of water one by one
In time can fill a giant pot.[12]

Three weeks into a weekly meditation course, a man came to speak to me. 'If I carry on with this,' he said, looking at me intently, 'doesn't it mean that I'm going to have to change my life?'

He'd already seen that if he seriously engaged with meditation it was going to have implications for his whole life. Meditation wasn't just something one did to unwind for half an hour at the end of the day, but a whole new way of living.

Taking up meditation doesn't necessarily entail living in a remote cave, or setting fire to our TV in a fit of renunciation. But if we are systematically cultivating awareness and loving-kindness, it is bound to have an effect on how we act on a day-to-day level. As we begin to enjoy a greater clarity of mind, we might start to resist aspects of our lives that detract from that awareness. Or we may start to notice emotional attitudes that are unhelpful, which might cause us to act in ways we regret, and we realize we want to revise them.

So we start making changes. Sometimes we do this without noticing – it just happens automatically. For example, we realize that formerly when we ate our breakfast, we would have listened to the radio while we read the paper. Now we only read the paper, or listen to the radio, but not both. We notice that these days we prefer to be without too much distraction around us.

Sometimes the change is more of a deliberate choice, yet it still comes easily and naturally. We might decide, for instance, to drink less alcohol because we've noticed that it doesn't help our meditation the following morning. In the event, we are surprised how little we miss it.

At other times, we decide to make a change that involves a bit more of a wrench, but we do it anyway. Although part of us resists, there is enough of us behind doing it to make it seem like a good idea. For example, when we have done the loving-kindness meditation for a while, we may feel we want to be vegetarian, but we also know we will miss eating meat. So perhaps we decide to change our diet over a period of time, say by not eating meat but still eating fish for a while.

In other words, we start lifting the practice away from the meditation cushion and spreading it more widely into our daily lives. We increasingly want to be able to act on the basis of the positive states of mind that we are cultivating in meditation. We aspire to change ourselves, move away from habits that limit us, and become better able to embody awareness and embrace loving-kindness. We want, if we can, to have a more positive effect on the world. Taking awareness and loving-kindness into our lives and out into the world is the practice of ethics. This chapter considers the Buddhist approach to ethics.

exercise – *what about ethics?*

Take a few minutes to consider your thoughts, feelings, and associations with the idea of being ethical. What does this mean to you? Does it sound pious and off-putting? Or is it necessary, but dull? Or do you find the idea interesting, even inspiring? Jot down any responses as they occur to you.

buddhist ethics

It is worth reflecting on our predisposition to the idea of an ethical life, since we often, I think, inherit from our surrounding culture a seriously impoverished view of what ethics is about. Or sometimes we have negative associations with the idea of ethics and morality because our previous experience was of it being inculcated in us in a narrow or dogmatic way. I've frequently noticed upon meeting someone and their discovering I'm a Buddhist, their first question is something like, 'What does that mean you're not allowed to do, then?' or, 'Does that mean you're not allowed to drink?' They identify ethics with rules, and with not being allowed to do what you want.

My reply to their questions is that as a Buddhist I can do whatever I like. However, I might *choose* to do, or not do, some things because of the effects I know they will have on me and on others. Buddhist ethics is not a list of rules and regulations, but about trying to make wise and aware choices. In the last two chapters we looked at meditation as the cultivation of positive frames of mind: those of mindfulness and loving-kindness. The practice of ethics involves acting in ways that are motivated by these qualities. If we do this, certain consequences follow. First, the positive frame of mind that we've acted from is reinforced. We are cultivating happiness for ourselves. Secondly, it has a much more positive effect on the world than if we had acted on the basis of a negative frame of mind. We are also cultivating happiness for others.

In other words, we could say that we are trying to bring creativity to our actions, in the sense of bringing awareness into our interactions with the world, instead of acting in the same tired, habitual, irritable, or busy way. When we are being creative, in the sense the word is being used here, we bring something new to the situation. We are more able to rise above a difficult situation. Whatever happens, we will try to be creative; to do so becomes deeply part of who we are. Someone like the Dalai Lama seems to be creative in this way. To all the troubles his people have faced under Chinese occupation, he could have easily – and understandably – responded with hatred or anger. But he seems to rise above the situation and encourage others to respond peacefully and with equanimity. This example has inspired many people all over the world.

Put another way, happiness is not something you can 'get' if only your life would work out just right. Happiness is a by-product of an aware and creative approach to life. It is this creativity that is the true source of happiness and contentment. That's why you can sometimes meet someone who has everything materially, but still doesn't seem satisfied. Or, you may meet someone whose life circumstances are hard, who undergoes suffering, but they meet it with an inner richness and optimism that is uplifting to witness. Despite their difficulties, they seem to be happy.

Ethics is the day-to-day implementation of this creative and responsive attitude to the world. We are attempting to be able to introduce awareness and clarity where there is confusion, understanding and sympathy where there is irritation, generosity where there is the pushing and shoving of too busy a world.

As we develop an ethical sensibility, we see more and more how we always dwell in possibility, how each moment contains choices and opportunities for such creativity. It is interesting to note that the traditional Buddhist Pali words that denote whether an act is ethical or unethical (*kusala* and *akusala*) mean 'skilful' and 'unskilful'. So ethical practice involves developing a *skill*. For example, if someone has to give criticism that they know the recipient will find difficult, it requires an intention of loving-kindness, but also skilled communication and qualities of tact and sensitivity. Thus it is something that we can learn and improve upon.

The tendency to see ethics in terms of rules has, unfortunately, gained a real hold in our culture. Sometimes when you talk to people about non-violence, they immediately want to know what you'd do if an evil dictator was about to press the button to start nuclear war and you just happen to be in the same room as them with a gun in your hand. They're really hoping they can catch you out by having to admit there might be circumstances in which you would need to use violence. They're interpreting, and they think you are interpreting, ethics in terms of black-and-white regulations, absolute rules. But ethics are principles to be applied in a complex world alongside other important principles and considerations.

Deciding between the death of a megalomaniac or nuclear holocaust is thankfully not a choice I'm confronted with on a daily basis. There are, however, dozens of occasions each day when I could choose to act with more awareness, or greater kindness. It is here that ethics comes into play. Discussions of ethics are often couched in terms of 'What would you do if X happened?' But perhaps a better question would be 'What kind of person do I want to become?' It is more important to develop the good qualities with which to make ethical decisions, than to know all the rights and wrongs of specific situations.

If we notice ourselves relating to ethics in terms of fixed rules, we may need to free ourselves of this mindset. On the other hand, it can be helpful to have ethical guidelines. They help us to be conscious of our ethical values, to remember those values and bear them in mind from day to day. These guidelines become benchmarks that we use to train ourselves, to develop more skill in the ethical sphere. They become a part of our way of life.

exercise – *living on a desert island*

This is an exercise I've sometimes done in groups, but you can try it as a reflection to do on your own.

Imagine you are stranded on a desert island with several other people, and you are together devising guidelines on how you should behave towards each other. What five guidelines would you suggest to your fellow islanders? Formulate them and write them down. Try to come up with your personal response, what you believe is most important, rather than repeat ethical guidelines you have come across elsewhere (including Buddhist ones). Do you find it easy or difficult to come up with ideas? Later, you can compare your list with the traditional Buddhist guidelines, such as the five precepts discussed below. Are there overlaps and similarities? Are there notable differences?

No matter how many times I've seen this exercise repeated in different groups of people, there is a noticeable overlap in the guidelines among the different groups. This suggests that, even if we are not fully conscious of them, we do have ethical values that inform our lives. We have a strong intuitive sense of ethics.

There is a set of guidelines in the Buddhist tradition known as the five precepts. The rest of this chapter will be a brief exploration of these. You'll see that each has a negative form – what it is we are trying to avoid – and a positive form: how we are trying to act. Because the discussion will be brief, we won't be looking at some of the more complex dilemmas facing the world, such as ecological questions, or the desirability of genetic engineering. Many of these issues do require exploration from an ethical point of view but, for now, we are trying to capture the spirit of each precept and how it might manifest in ordinary life.

As we've already seen, these precepts are not rules, but principles we are trying to bring into effect. It is not the letter that is important, but the spirit and intention behind them. They are about developing skilfulness in our interactions with the world. Developing a skill takes practice. Like meditation, the ethical precepts are a practice. 'Precept' in this context means 'training principle'. We gradually learn through experience and practice how to embody more awareness and love in the world.

not taking life, not harming, and acting with loving-kindness

The negative form of this first precept is not to take life or cause harm; the positive form is to act with loving-kindness. This precept emphasizes the need to try to be aware of others' needs. It is concerned with putting the loving-kindness meditation into action in everyday life. Our intentions of kindness and well-wishing need to be acted on and made real – otherwise it can just become somewhat sentimental or abstract.

When we manage to respond to people's needs, they usually notice and appreciate it. There was once a lady who came to our Buddhist centre who was in rather an unhappy state. She would talk at you incessantly about nothing in particular. Eventually she got it into her head that we Buddhists should open a vegetarian restaurant. She would phone up and, if we weren't there, leave messages with soup recipes on our answering machine. Sometimes the messages would last for half an hour and use up all the tape.

One day she caught me on the phone and started to launch into another recipe. I felt myself tensing up with irritation. Just at that moment, I managed to understand what it was she really wanted. 'But Ruth,' I said, cutting across her, 'How are *you*?'

There was a long silence. Then a sad and sorry voice started to tell me about her difficulties, her sick mother, and her own history of mental illness. Just for a few moments I'd been able to relate to her need to talk to someone. I'd got underneath the hopelessly mistaken strategy of non-stop talking she'd devised for trying to meet her need to communicate. Probably it was only rarely that someone asked her how she was. We'd broken through into real human communication.

How can we live our lives so that we help others to be enriched, expanded, and to be more human, rather than to be lessened or taken for granted? Can we think of appropriate practical activities? They might be large or small, but that doesn't matter. This is the challenge of the first precept. This precept is the most important, in the sense that it contains the principle of non-harm and loving-kindness that underlies all the other precepts. The remaining four precepts can be seen as consequences of the first, almost as applications of this precept to other areas of life.

not taking the not-given, and acting with generosity

The wording 'not taking the not-given' of this precept is revealing. It doesn't just suggest not stealing, but that we don't take anything unless we know it has been freely given. In other words, it is encouraging a non-exploitative approach to life.

We might, for example, try to act in ways that we think will minimize harm to the environment, or we might try to buy fair-trade goods. There are also smaller instances of the same attitude of not taking advantage, such as not borrowing things from our friends without asking, and making sure we return borrowed items on time and in good condition.

Although we might not steal big things, or take from people we know, we might sometimes take small items from workplaces or institutions. For example, we help ourselves to some office stationery. We tell ourselves it is owed to us. We actually feel this – that life owes us a living. (You can see this attitude at work in such small instances, but also in larger cases of theft or fraud.) But if we think about it, we see that this is a self-centred attitude. We are putting our own needs above everyone else.

One day a beggar comes up to me in the high street and asks for some money. From over the road I've seen him approaching me. I've immediately started to feel uncomfortable and started to look the other way. I'm pretending to be fascinated by those ladies' handbags in the shop window. But why is this? Putting aside for a moment all the arguments about whether you should give money to a beggar if he might spend it on drink, why do I feel such a resistance? If I did give him a coin from my pocket, I suspect that when I got my change out an hour later I wouldn't even notice the missing cash. Why do I feel such a resistance to giving away something I'm not even going to miss?

The resistance occurs because we feel that we can't spare anything. We have a sense of inner poverty and lack. We think the world owes us, but we cannot give anything.

However, when we are generous, there is a sense of inner richness and abundance. We are able to relate to the world in a different way, more in terms of 'what can I give?' rather than an attitude of 'what can I get?' We can perhaps reflect on this ourselves: at what times and situations do we find it easier to give? When, on the other hand, do we find it more difficult?

People are very generous much of the time. In a way, generosity is innate and natural. You may have had an experience which meant a lot to you, or that was really enjoyable. You will often be eager to tell someone about it. You naturally want to share it with your friends. We want to be connected to others and this can mean we want to give and share with them. We enjoy giving gifts and watching the pleasure of the recipient. There are plenty of other examples of people really giving of themselves to help another. A friend of mine once went travelling in India with his girlfriend, who then became very ill. He tried to buy a train ticket to get her to a hospital in a city, but was told no tickets were available for many days. They were both anxious and frightened in a strange country where they didn't know who to trust. A young Muslim man befriended them and offered to help. Could they trust him? They decided to take the risk and he spent many hours at the train station queuing for tickets and insisting they be allowed to travel soon. He eventually got the tickets, but wouldn't accept anything by way of thanks. He just saw two people in need and decided to give his time and help.

avoiding sexual misconduct – stillness, simplicity, and contentment

Why does sex get a precept to itself? Not because there is anything inherently sinful about sex, but because there is something inherently dangerous about it. Our sex life draws out some of our strongest desires, and it is here that we are often at our most intimate, and therefore vulnerable. So the potential to do harm, or be hurt, is increased.

This precept extends the first and second precepts into the arena of sexuality. It asks that we do not hurt or exploit through sexual relationships. This covers the obvious and extreme instances, such as rape, but we can also look at more subtle levels of the precept.

Our culture seems obsessed with sex. It is used to sell everything and anything. Acres of newsprint are given to sniggering at the sex lives of the famous, while magazine articles explain how to spice up your own sex life. As a culture, we're in reaction to an era of sexual repression; it seems we're trying to make up for lost time. But maybe we've just gone from one extreme to another. The third precept asks that we free ourselves from these cultural influences: there is no need to feel guilty about sex, nor do we have to go along with the current over-obsession.

Sex is natural, human, and can be very pleasurable, but we should not over-value it. Sometimes we get out of touch with ourselves and we feel empty inside. We look for something outside us to fill that gap. Sex is one of the things we turn to. So it is not that there is anything wrong with a healthy sex life, but we do not want to rely too heavily on, or be addicted to, sex.

The positive form of this precept is to practise stillness, simplicity, and contentment. Contentment is not an emotionally dry and withered state, but one of inner richness in which one does not need to look outside oneself for emotional satisfaction. It is not a state of non-emotion. A contented person might still feel passionately about some things. They have passion, but they do not let passion have them. In some religious institutions today, you hear of people who are celibate, but clearly they are not content. They seem emotionally restricted, lonely, and unhappy. This is not a good advertisement for the states of contentment that are possible when we are deeply in touch with our vision and sources of emotional fulfilment. In the Buddhist tradition, the word for celibacy is *brahmacarya*, which literally means 'dwelling with the gods', which gives you a sense of what is meant by true contentment. It is a state of happiness and pleasure. We develop contentment not just by giving up that which is pleasurable, but also by refining our pleasures. We look for what gives us the deepest, truest satisfaction.

We can perhaps watch ourselves. Are there situations and times in which we are particularly content, and others in which we are prone to craving and restlessness? For example, I know that if I've been busy for too long and have lost touch with my inner inspiration, or lost my sense of connection with others, this is when I start to feel empty inside. Then I start craving something to fill the gap, and often think about sex more than usual. On the other hand, when I'm inspired, or enjoying open communication with others, or when I'm on retreat, I think about sex much less, and I feel more deeply content. Once we become aware of these patterns in ourselves, we can try to ensure we take time to cultivate pleasure and contentment.

avoid false speech, communicate truthfully
The fourth precept asks us to communicate truthfully. Before we can speak the truth to others, we need to be in contact with the truth ourselves. Truthfulness is an inner attitude, as well as an outer quality. As we go about our lives, we tell ourselves a story, we interpret and process our experience internally. We need to do this. We need to construct for ourselves a healthy sense of who we are in relation to the world. But sometimes, if we look closely – and this may even shock us – we find we are telling ourselves a lie. We subtly tell ourselves a version of reality that shows us in a good light. We don't want to admit, even to ourselves, that we act unkindly, that we have ungenerous thoughts, or that other people sometimes get the better of us.

One of the great qualities connected with truthfulness is authenticity – being seen as we truly are. To be authentic is no small achievement – it takes a great deal of courage and confidence and may take some time to develop. The first stage in being authentic is to be so with oneself. Only then can we be authentic with others. The more we have this quality, the freer we are. When we are not afraid to be seen as we are, others cannot manipulate us.

When we don't speak the truth, it is often because we want to be seen in a good light. We don't exactly blame our colleagues for the mistake we make, but we omit to put our boss right when they assume it was someone else that was in the wrong. Or we exaggerate the details of a story we are telling because we want to impress. Sometimes, when you overhear a conversation between friends, it sounds more like a competition in which each is trying to trump the other with a better story, or a funnier joke. There is very little real communication. You might say that a little bit of exaggeration isn't that serious. From one point of view it isn't, but, on the other hand, it is a missed opportunity to be more truly ourselves, rather than merely keep up the pretence.

Ethically skilful communication involves more than just factual truth. To quote William Blake, 'A truth that's told with bad intent, beats all the lies you can invent.'[13] We are trying to communicate not just truthfully, but also with loving-kindness. We try to avoid harsh, unkind comments. I once heard about a woman who worked in an office where there was a lot of gossip behind someone's back. She was eventually asked what she thought of that person. She replied that she knew she had plenty of faults herself, so she tried not to dwell on the faults of others. The gossip stopped.

When you are with someone who habitually speaks kindly and appreciatively of others it is very uplifting. I have a friend with whom I spend time every few weeks. When I was first getting to know him, I noticed that each time I returned home I would almost feel inspired, and I'd wonder why. We'd only chatted about ordinary things. I realized it was because he always spoke in a positive and appreciative manner. Negative words poison the atmosphere, but positive words are just as potent in having the opposite effect.

avoiding intoxicants, acting with mindfulness
This final precept is about taking mindfulness into everyday life. It suggests we avoid anything that intoxicates, or detracts from, our mindfulness. We have to decide for ourselves what these things are, and where we want to draw the line. We might find that we can have the odd drink without affecting our awareness too much, or we might decide that even one glass of wine mars our clarity. Our experience might be that there are other things that detract from our mindfulness. For example, we find that spending too long in front of the computer spaces us out. Again, there are no hard and fast rules, but a principle that we have to apply in the world.

However, one could argue that a strong characteristic of our culture is our over-reliance of drink and drugs. Karen Armstrong, a writer on comparative religion, has recently suggested that many are seeking ecstasy through drink, drugs, sport, sex, dancing and clubbing, art, and even shopping.[14] We are looking for an experience that takes us out of ourselves. This is natural, and what humans have always sought. In the past, many did this through religious experience, but these traditions have today lost their vitality. Much contemporary religion has lost touch with its mystical roots, and may even be suspicious of them. So today we use different means. The problem is that this is often not grounded in ethics. This can lead some people to dependence on, or addiction to, drugs, or to the violence one sometimes sees on the football terraces. Also, the satisfaction it can give us just doesn't go very deep, nor does it last very long. This is because true ecstasy is a product of a way of being, not something we consume. So we either have ethics that is wary of ecstasy (much contemporary religion), or ecstasy not grounded in ethics (much of modern culture). Karen Armstrong suggests that the current western interest in Buddhism is connected to this search for an ecstasy that is firmly grounded in ethics.

With this precept, we are also exploring the whole area of mindfulness in everyday life as discussed in Chapter 2. If we are not mindful, we cannot be aware of our actions, words, and underlying motives. In other words, mindfulness is the necessary condition for practising the other precepts, for dwelling more fully in the possibilities of our lives, for bringing more loving-kindness into the world.

developing a ethical life

Even from this brief discussion, we can see that the scope of ethics is wide and deep. Most of us probably do not act in ways that are grossly unskilful, but there are still many ways in which we could more fully put these precepts into effect. With experience, we come to develop and refine our ethical sensibility. We see more vividly the significance of our actions, and we want to bring out the best in ourselves and bring more good into the world. This does not mean being all prim and pious. If we notice ourselves becoming self-righteous, we have probably lost touch with the spirit of the precept and are relating to it as a rule.

On the other hand, we might notice that we can be apathetic or slap-dash, thinking our behaviour will make no difference. But even if we are unsure whether an action will have much positive impact in the world, we might want to do it anyway. Our attitude and intentions have an importance all of their own. For example, we might recycle paper, even though we're not really sure whether it will make any difference to the environment when there are so many tons of paper produced each day. But just acting out of care for the world, rather than acting carelessly and unmindfully, has its own value. It is the expression of a positive frame of mind that then helps to safeguard and reinforce an attitude of concern and awareness.

As we practise the precepts, we learn more about ourselves, our strengths and our weaknesses, our habits and our inclinations. We gradually refine our practice and develop more awareness of exactly which aspect of a given precept we most need to work upon. For example, we begin by wanting to be more kind, but we gradually learn about ourselves and more precisely what we find easy and what we find difficult about being kind. This gives us a more exact sense of how to work with the precept. In a way, the precepts are quite general and we need to formulate a more specific precept, resolution, or 'training principle' that is particular to us. To say we want to be 'more kind' is very vague. We need to ask *when and where* we want to do this, towards *whom* we want to be more kind, and exactly *how* that kindness would manifest itself. Unless our sense of what we are working on is sufficiently specific, it won't have much effect on our ethical practice, but if we can identify an achievable goal for ourselves, we realize that we really can change.

exercise – *formulating our own precept*

Sitting quietly, and allowing plenty of time, go back over all five precepts and choose one that you would like to work on and develop further. Jot down your response to each of the following questions:

In what situations am I at my best in this matter? When is it that I find it most difficult?

What is it about this precept that I do well? In what areas could I practise the precept more fully? Are there areas where I fall down?

Then, based on these reflections, develop your own precept, your own particular application of one of the five. Try to be specific about what it is you intend to change. Try also to be realistic and choose something concrete and achievable!

You might come back to this exercise a week later and reflect on how you got on with your particular precept. Do you want to continue working with it, or adapt and refine it further?

You could eventually work with all the precepts in this way, trying to see how they apply to your own life. Through such practice, they become something we remember and relate to more automatically and spontaneously.

The above discussion has introduced each precept very briefly. We have to be aware that the world is complex and in our application of the precepts we need to act intelligently and be patient with ourselves. There will not always be one clear course of action, but competing choices in which we'll need to weigh up how best to respond. Or a situation might arise very quickly and not leave us much time to decide how to act. The practice of ethics is about acknowledging complexity, but doing the best we can, and being prepared to learn from our experience.

The way we experience the world is a product of the actions of those that live in it. I once rented a cottage in rural south-west Ireland. The owner, as he gave me the key, told me I didn't need to bother locking up when I went out. They never had burglaries round there. This had a strong effect on me. I realized that there was a low-level, underlying anxiety that comes with having to constantly remember locks and keys, and worry about getting robbed. Living in a city involves living all the time with an insidious, underlying fear and mistrust. It was a relief to drop all that for a couple of weeks. It showed me how we tend to get used to the world being a certain way, so we stop noticing how we are constantly affected by each other's actions. Even if we are lucky enough not to be burgled, we are still influenced by living in a world in which such things occur.

As well as reflecting on how negative actions affect the world directly and indirectly, we can also reflect on the converse of this: how a better world requires people more inspired and motivated by an ethical vision. A more compassionate society can only arise when individual people are more compassionate.

In the first exercise of this chapter we looked at our underlying attitudes to ethics and how, in western society, the idea of ethics can often be degraded. But, actually, the practice of ethics can be, should be, fascinating, challenging, and inspiring. It is about building a better world.

5

right livelihood
chopping wood, fetching water

Water to draw
brushwood to cut
greens to pick –
all in moments when
morning showers let up.[15]

When they encounter Buddhism and meditation for the first time, some people feel it rekindles something deep within them, something that may have been lying dormant for a very long time. In the busyness of everyday affairs we can lose contact with that deeper sense of ourselves and the potential creativity of our lives. But the inner spaciousness we discover in meditation brings back the feeling of dwelling in possibility. We may feel we have rediscovered something precious that we don't want lose sight of again.

But then we wonder whether, with our current life and responsibilities, it is possible to stay in touch with all this. Can we fully implement Buddhist ideals and really change ourselves? Can we really make significant progress in the midst of bringing up a family, or a busy job, or both? Can we do it in a world driven by consumerism, which seems intent on distracting us? Or is serious practice only for those who can go and live in the mountains, far away from worldly concerns?

exercise – *is it really possible for me?*
Take a few moments to sit quietly and consider the above questions, and unravel your feelings and beliefs as to whether the

path of self-transformation is possible for you. Try to be just as honest in acknowledging your underlying attitudes, regardless of whether they express doubt or confidence. You might find they are a mixture of the two.

Another question that might help you to think about this is, 'What prevents me from practising more fully? What holds me back from making more progress in meditation, ethics, and the process of self-transformation?'

Make notes about your responses to these questions.

It is important to know because, if we are subconsciously telling ourselves it is not possible, this will obviously influence the effectiveness of our practice!

This chapter concerns itself with such questions. We'll be looking at how we *can* live a radical and meaningful spiritual life in the midst of the world, and how this can, in fact, be a strong and effective way of practising. But we'll also be considering the supportive conditions we need to maintain the depth and momentum of such practice. In other words, we'll be trying to get some sense of what a Buddhist lifestyle might look like. We'll see that it involves learning to combine both calm and activity. We will also explore the topic of 'right livelihood': how to approach working life from the point of view of Buddhist ideals.

But first, we will look at some areas of conflict that can arise as we start to get more involved in the Buddhist life. Perhaps we have been attending a Buddhism class for a few months, we find we enjoy meditation, and notice we that we are starting to change. We begin to make friends at the class, and appreciate the contact with people who think and feel as we do. But we are also worried about certain questions. Isn't it selfish to be spending so much time meditating? How can you justify all that time for yourself? What will your family think? Is this meditation business just a form of escapism? Do your friends secretly worry that you've gone weird and joined a cult? Do they even think that you'll soon be clearing out the bank account and disappearing in the middle of the night to join some mystical guru with seventeen Rolls-Royces? (Maybe you recognize versions of these, or similar areas of conflict and uncertainty?)

Some people do seem to worry that meditation is a bit selfish. The fact that it involves taking time out and going into our inner world leads some people to feel guilty about meditating. But if we are doing it in order to live our lives better, in order to interact with the world with more awareness and loving-kindness, then it is far from selfish. It is an investment in ourselves now, so that we have more to give later: not necessarily more in the quantitative sense, but in enabling ourselves to do what we do with a better quality of mind. This will affect how well we are able to do it. Such an investment is wise, not selfish.

Meditation is the exact opposite of escapism. Escapism is avoiding oneself – perhaps by losing oneself in an activity that allows us to forget our lives. But when we meditate we are looking into our minds and trying to be aware and honest about what we see. We are taking responsibility for our minds in a radical and uncompromising way. Meditation is a challenge, but a worthwhile and rewarding one.

Anne Donovan has written a funny and perceptive novel called *Buddha Da*.[16] It is the story of a Glaswegian family: Jimmy, a painter and decorator, his wife Liz, and their daughter Anne-Marie. Jimmy has become interested in meditation and started going along to the Buddhist centre. At first, Anne-Marie wonders whether it is just one of his practical jokes, but she gradually realizes he is serious. She and her mother find it weird that dad, who used to spend his evenings sitting with them watching telly and cracking jokes, now goes upstairs to sit for hours on his own in a darkened room. Liz cannot understand why Jimmy comes home from the centre in such awe of what the lama said that night. To her, it sounds little different to what the priest says on Sunday – but Jimmy has never been interested in church. Anne-Marie's religious education class at school goes on a visit to the Buddhist centre and she is in terror of the potential embarrassment: what if her dad is there, or one of the lamas recognizes her? You can see that something has awoken in Jimmy, albeit imperfectly – he is at times rather oblivious of the effects he is having on his family. He struggles to explain why it is so vitally important to him, but he can't quite put it into words. Mutual incomprehension abounds, and the novel goes on to tell us the results.

Where there is such conflict and difficulty, we usually, in time, work through it. In the end, relationships are often stronger and closer as a result. My parents were understandably wary when I got involved in Buddhism. They had brought me up as a Roman Catholic and must have wondered why I was rejecting that faith. They had done their best to explain and teach me their faith – why wasn't it good enough for me? In time, however, they saw that I was happy and that what I was doing suited me. They are now very supportive of my Buddhist life, and I feel very close to them and grateful for all they have done for me. My father sometimes comes and stays with me in the Buddhist community where I live, and I am glad he's able to get a closer glimpse of my life in this way.

Sometimes, however, such a resolution and understanding is not possible: friends or partners realize that their paths through life are diverging. They simply have different goals and aims, so they may decide to part. Though this is sometimes sad and painful, they feel it will be better for all concerned in the long run.

How can we negotiate this difficult territory? There are obviously no easy answers or simple formulas. We first need to be aware that if we start getting involved in meditation and Buddhism, it might seem strange to people who are close to us but don't share our interest. They might not be able to understand why it is meaningful to us. It might even seem alien and threatening to them; they fear our new interest will come between us and them. We need to attempt to understand this and to communicate what meditation and practice is all about and why it is significant for us. We do our best to help them understand. At the same time, we try not to ignore the call of our heart, even when it causes difficulty for others. We can only remain true to others if we are first true to ourselves, so we try to listen to that voice within that tells us how we really want to live our lives.

buddhist lifestyles

We could say, putting it simply, that there are two ways of practising, two basic Buddhist lifestyles. One could be called 'practice in the world', and the other, 'practice apart from the world'.

Practice in the world means living in the midst of society. Maybe we have a job, or we're bringing up a family, or we continue participating in society in some other way. But we are also, at the same time, trying to put Buddhist teachings and practices into effect.

Practice apart from the world means we leave society to some extent. Perhaps we live in a retreat centre in the countryside, or a monastery, or a hermitage. We have deliberately isolated ourselves from the world in order to be able to concentrate solely on Buddhist practice. We spend as much of our time as possible in this environment, leaving it only when we need to.

Both these are valid forms of practice that have been present in Buddhist traditions right from the start. The Buddha left society in order to pursue a spiritual quest. He went deep into the forests to seek out spiritual teachers and to meditate on the mysteries of existence. This is often the popular image of the Buddha: a solitary, meditating figure.

But that was not the whole story. After the Buddha gained Enlightenment, he returned to the world. He travelled all over north-east India, teaching and communicating his experience of Enlightenment, so that others could experience that freedom for themselves. He founded an order, so that his followers could support each other in their practice, and so that his teaching could be passed from generation to generation. The organization of this order, and all the teaching, meant he was a busy man. As he travelled around, he would often have been accompanied by a retinue of followers, with hundreds of people coming to hear him talk and ask questions. He also went back to his family, and many of them became his followers – some also gaining Enlightenment. He met and taught all sorts of people, from a wide variety of backgrounds.

So we can see that there was a stage in his life when the Buddha did practise apart from the world, but then he returned. We can see both ways of functioning exemplified in his life.

The wide range of people taught by the Buddha also practised in a variety of ways. Some followed his earlier example and went into the forest to explore the depths of meditation. Some remained in their lay lifestyles, but still pursued the spiritual life and made substantial progress. Some became renunciants, living on the outskirts of towns and villages, but travelling into them to gather food from the laypeople, give teachings, and conduct the business of the order.

It is much the same today. There are a variety of ways in which we can follow the path. Each will have particular strengths and potential dangers. When finding a way to practise, it is also a question of finding what suits our temperament. It is not the case that what is right for one person will work for all. It is important to realize this, otherwise we may become discouraged. Sometimes we see that a person who teaches Buddhism has a different lifestyle from us – one that we could not follow. Perhaps they live with other Buddhists and go on retreat a lot, whereas we have a busy family life. So we start thinking that practising in our situation is impossible, and we become despondent. Or we might be genuinely impressed with the teacher's qualities and attributes, so we think we should be able to be like them. But then we find we can't – our temperament and talents are just different. We have to find our own way – a path that suits our particular abilities and character. This just takes time.

Many people, when they come across the Buddhist path, have responsibilities such as family that they cannot, and do not wish to, leave. So most people pursuing Buddhism in the West are probably going to be practising 'in the world'. One advantage of this mode of practice is that the world will keep you on your toes! If we are active in the world, ethical challenges are guaranteed. We encounter people we find difficult, and there are multiple demands on our time and generosity. Although we might wish at times that these problems would all go away, they can be challenges that spur us on to develop. Without them, we might not make much effort in our meditation. This is my experience. It is often when life is difficult, and I'm struggling, that I'm most motivated in meditation. At these times I know I *have* to meditate – otherwise life will be hell! When times are easier, meditation can seem less of an imperative.

The danger inherent in practice in the world is that we can become overwhelmed by the world. We struggle to find the time to meditate, and when we do find it, our minds are so stimulated by the busyness of our day that our meditation seems hopeless. We find it too difficult to implement ethical ideals when surrounded by people who have no interest in them. Perhaps we are so immersed in the world that we even start to lose sight of those ideals ourselves.

With practice apart from the world it is the opposite. The strength of this approach is that we will not be swamped by the world. On the contrary, we have time and space to explore the spiritual life, relatively free from stress, worry, and distraction. We can do so in ideal conditions – perhaps in quiet, beautiful countryside, or with others who are doing the same thing and therefore support our efforts. We dwell in a place where everything is designed to remind us of, and support, our ideals and aspirations.

At the same time, unless we are sufficiently self-motivated and alive to the dangers, we might just tread water. We might be going through the motions in our practice, but our lives don't really challenge us, spur us on, or provide the medium in which we learn to consider the needs of others. In a way, it could become *too* supportive.

There is no perfect solution: however we choose to live the spiritual life, there will be opportunities and potential dangers. We just have to be aware of these, and negotiate the territory as best we can. Assuming that most people who will be reading this book will be practising in the world, most of what follows concerns that path.

the life of calm and activity

Hakuin was a Zen master who lived in eighteenth-century Japan. He was also a renowned painter and calligrapher, and some of his self-portraits survive to this day. They depict a large, formidable looking man, bald, with intense, bulging eyes, and a grizzly beard. He looks as though he could have tattoos under his robes and ride a motorbike at weekends. But Hakuin was very dedicated to his practice, and had some profound spiritual experiences during his life.

Two of the things Hakuin used to talk about were the 'life of activity' and the 'life of calm'.[17] In a way, what he meant by these phrases was similar to what we have been talking about as practice in the world and practice apart from the world. When leading an active life, it was obvious that one needed some calm to counterbalance it, and to help engage in activity with awareness and creativity. But Hakuin was also concerned that some of his disciples were choosing the life of calm for the wrong reasons. If they went to live in the mountains, it was because they had over-identified this lifestyle with the spiritual life. Or perhaps they were actually choosing it out of a desire to live somewhere peaceful and beautiful, rather than because they really wanted to make spiritual progress. He said they were often weak and incapable when they returned to the life of activity.

For Hakuin, the ideal was to blend a life of calm and a life of activity. Each was essential, but one without the other was useless. Activity and calm were to be practised together at deeper and deeper levels. So, when performing a task such as chopping wood, or fetching water, one would do it mindfully – almost like a meditation practice. One would stop making such hard and fast distinctions between calm and activity, and hankering for one or other.

In Zen circles there was a saying designed to depict the ordinary, down-to-earth quality of mindfulness. 'A monk who is really practising meditation knows he is walking when he is walking, and knows he is sitting (in meditation) when he is sitting.' Hakuin (who was a bit of a wit) played on this, saying, 'A monk who is really practising meditation does *not* know when he is walking and when he is sitting.' In other words, *everything* was potentially a practice – the monk ceased to make distinctions between what was practice, and what wasn't.

The lesson here is that we, too, need to blend the life of calm and the life of activity. How can we do this? We can look at how we can engage in our own life of activity as a practice in itself. We'll explore this below, when we look at right livelihood, and also in the next chapter when we encounter the 'worldly winds'.

But if we are leading an active life, we also need to ensure there are times of calm that counterbalance this and provide the conditions which creatively support engagement with the activity. To do this, we may want to make some changes to the way we live our lives. For example, we want to give enough attention to meditation, making it a priority and establishing a daily routine that makes time for it. We may value spending time with others who meditate and can support our efforts. We may also be able to go on retreat for a weekend, a week, or longer. Within the calmness of a retreat we can look back on the story of our lives and gain more clarity and perspective than might be possible while we are in the thick of it. Immersed in the more ideal conditions of a retreat we gain the confidence and inspiration to take our values much more seriously, to consider how we really want to be living life. We often leave a retreat feeling invigorated, with our practice recharged, and ready to re-engage with the life of activity.

I was once lucky enough to take part in a four-month retreat at a place called Guhyaloka in southern Spain. The name, which means 'secret realm', was certainly appropriate. Far into the mountains, the retreat centre is in an area of woodland surrounded by dramatic limestone cliffs. During the retreat we would sometimes climb up these cliffs so that, in effect, we formed a circle and faced each other across the valley. We would chant mantras as loud as we could and listen to them echoing and re-echoing around the valley walls. Part of the significance of the retreat was that we were indeed coming to a secret place. We had left our ordinary lives, our country and our homes, friends, work, family – all the things we normally rely on to give us a sense of who we are – far behind us. This is what is known traditionally as 'going forth'. It gives us a different experience of ourselves outside of our usual conditioning, which can be extremely valuable in finding out who we really are and who we want to be.

Towards the end of the retreat something else happened. At dusk we again went up on top of the valley walls, but this time we all faced outwards. The rock face was golden in the dying sunlight. The twinkling lights of towns and villages were starting to emerge in the distance. Each of us read favourite texts and inspirational verses out towards the world. We were doing this to signify that we were shortly going back to the world, and we wanted to take something back with us. We wanted to have something new to give once we returned to our familiar lives. This is what it is like with a retreat: you go away, but you do so in order to come back again.

Getting the right balance between calm and activity is far from easy. For most of us, the life of activity will probably take over, and we may feel we have lost sight of the life of calm! In fact, it might be rare that we get the balance exactly right. This is not a problem as long as we are aware of the dynamic and do what we can to right it. It is when the imbalance goes on for too long that we might run into trouble, such as stress or burnout. But gradually, through trial and error, we learn how to remain at least in some sense of contact with that inner spaciousness; we get to know our limits and how much busyness we can deal with before our practice becomes thin. It is like keeping a boat on course. We keep an eye on its direction, the wind, and the weather, and we turn the rudder. Sometimes we turn it strongly to bring about a big change of direction. Later, only small adjustments are needed to remain on course.

exercise – *calm and activity*

Sitting quietly for a few moments, begin to consider the balance of calm and activity in your life. Thinking about the following questions may help.

Are there times when the balance is tipped too far in favour of calm, or activity? What are the symptoms of this in how you feel internally and in how you engage with what you are doing?

Are there times when you feel you get the balance about right? What does that feel like?

If and when you lose balance, do you believe it is possible to restore it, taking into account your responsibilities? What is your underlying attitude or predisposition to this question?

Look at the question of balance once again. Perhaps there are small, practical changes that would make more difference than you expect to your inner sense of balance. Make a note of just one or two practical ideas that you could try to implement. (These might be things like going for a quiet walk in your lunch break, or not listening to the radio while you drink your morning cup of tea, but using that time to reflect.)

So perhaps the twofold model discussed above was rather too simplistic. It is not that we are either practising in the world or apart from the world. Although one mode might predominate, we have times when we are in the other. There is a relationship between these two modes in our lives. Even a twenty-minute meditation in the morning is like a little retreat: we leave the world behind for a short while, but we come back to it refreshed. We have a few moments of calm in order to prepare for the activity of the day.

It was the same with the Buddha. Although, as we have seen, he returned to the world after his Enlightenment, he still went back to the forests to meditate. The order he founded was an attempt to create a new lifestyle that was both within, and apart from, the world. The monks and nuns had plenty of time and support for practice, but they also played a role in society – teaching others about the path to Enlightenment.

As well as ensuring we have adequate calm, such as our daily meditation that prepares us for the activity of the day, we also need to learn how to make our active lives part of our practice. We are trying to develop awareness and loving-kindness as much of the time as possible, not only in meditation. This brings us to the topic of work as practice.

right livelihood

The Buddha taught what he called the Noble Eightfold Path – eight specific areas of practice that together constitute the path to Enlightenment. The fifth of these is right livelihood, and we'll consider the process of bringing the practice of awareness and loving-kindness into our lives of activity under this heading.

A friend of mine, when discussing work and spiritual practice, especially if people were complaining about difficulties in their jobs, used to give the following advice. He said that if, by the end of the week, we couldn't think of one good reason for doing our job, we should leave.

Life is short and precious. Why do something for eight hours a day, five days a week, forty-something weeks a year for the rest of our lives, if we don't know why we are doing it? Especially when you take into account the idea of karma – that the kind of person we become is a product of the choices and actions we take all day – we can see that work and livelihood is a vital spiritual issue.

Sometimes we do make big changes to our lives because we realize our heart is no longer in what we are doing. This can take courage, especially when we are no longer young, but it may be well worth it. I have one friend who for many years was a stressed-out administrator in the National Health Service. He eventually decided to change direction, retrained, and became much happier giving careers advice to young people.

On the other hand, we might realize there *are* good reasons why we do our job. These might be many and varied, or it might simply be that we are doing the job because we need the money to support our family. But that is still a positive reason. If we are clear about our reasons for doing something, it can help us feel much better about doing it.

Here, we'll look at four basic elements of right livelihood. These are four suggested areas with which to consider to what extent our working life constitutes right livelihood. Does our work give us what we need under each of these four headings?

support

First, we need work that gives us adequate financial support, work that is enjoyable, and that allows us to be part of society. We do need a reasonable level of income for ourselves and those for whom we are financially responsible. This might require a full-time job, or we might change our priorities and work part time. We might be happy to earn less because we value the time this makes available for other activities.

Whatever we do, it is important that we stay emotionally alive. We need something in our lives that draws out the best in us. If this isn't in our work, we must find it in another aspect of our lives. Our emotional energy needs somewhere to flow. Sometimes we meet people who have been stuck in a rut for years, trundling along on the same old lines. It is as if something inside has been snuffed out. It is a sad waste of potential. As much as we can, we should 'follow our bliss'. We should do what we love, while also remembering our responsibilities to others.

In many faith traditions, work is seen as a vital aspect of being healthy and human. Most of us need an activity that brings forth our energies and talents, and through which we can make a contribution to society. Through our work we can experience ourselves as part of society. We learn about our interconnectedness as human beings, how we need to give and take.

benefiting others

The second way in which our work can become right livelihood is by ensuring that it is ethical and of benefit to the world. I often notice that people who take up meditation are already employed in right livelihood in this sense. They have taken up jobs that obviously benefit other people. Once we have been meditating for a while, it often becomes even more important to us that our work accords with our altruistic ideals.

But even if our work is not the kind that we usually think of as socially useful, it will still contain opportunities to benefit others. For example, if we are more emotionally positive, calm, and collected, this will have a transforming effect on everyone in our workplace. Most work involves provision of a service or a product, so we can try to provide the best service to others. Or we might give some of our earnings to charities and social projects. Many faiths have a tradition of tithing a proportion of one's income in this way. A friend of mine used to give a day's earnings per month to a good cause. On a certain day each month he would remind himself that he wasn't just working for himself, but for the benefit of others.

supportive of our practice

Thirdly, for a job to constitute right livelihood, it needs to be part of, and support, our spiritual practice. As my Buddhist teacher once said, 'Unless your work is your meditation, your meditation is not meditation.'[18] Whatever your job, it will contain opportunities to cultivate more mindfulness, chances to develop loving-kindness, ways of interacting with others more ethically. This is what is meant by making your work your meditation. Issues will arise that pose spiritual challenges for us: how can we respond to that awkward colleague with loving-kindness? What do we do if our boss has asked us to conceal something from a customer? These may not be easy issues, but they are the stuff of the real spiritual life.

It might be easy to find ways of making our work part of our practice. Or it may be that we decide that circumstances at work are too stressful, or the people we work with unsupportive, and we consider a change to work that will be more conducive to our practice.

Some Buddhists have approached this issue by establishing businesses or ventures in which they can work together as a team. The hope is that they can then really explore what it means for work to be a spiritual practice, together with others who are committed to the same ideals. This can bring about a strong sense of shared purpose, communication, and co-operation.

Work (along with meditation and friendship) can be used as one of the most powerful tools for changing ourselves. Because it demands our energy and skill, it can draw us out and transform us. We learn about our limitations, are spurred to develop new abilities, and can then grow in confidence. This is my experience of work. I'm lucky to work at a Buddhist centre; my work is very much intertwined with my ideals and practice. But my job there has been a crucial part of that practice. Most of what I've learned and changed about myself has been through work. For example, I've had to learn to think much more for myself, to respond with equanimity to criticism or blame, to deal with difficulties in communication, and to develop more confidence in my own vision.

simplicity

Buddhists talk a lot about contentment and simplicity, but what do these ideals actually amount to when we are in the midst of a busy job? What does simplicity mean in a society that is complex, quick to change, technologically sophisticated, and far from simple?

Maybe simplicity is about doing what is really important in our lives and not getting caught up in that which is of lesser importance. There is a well-known exercise in which participants are asked to write down all their plans for the coming year. (If you want to do this exercise yourself, then don't read any further before you've done that bit!) Then they are given a second sheet of paper and asked to write their plans for the year once again, but this time knowing that it is the last year of their life. The contents of the two sheets are often very different – the hopes and aims of the first suddenly appear in a new perspective. This exercise might show us what is really important and worth focusing on.

So we do not have to ignore or avoid the complex and sophisticated society in which we live. We can benefit from the possibilities it allows. But we make use of those possibilities, rather than letting them use us. I run a lot of weekend retreats as part of my work at the Buddhist centre. I've noticed something about them over the last few years. In the old days, people would arrive on Friday night, stay for the weekend, and return home on Sunday. These days, people arrive, phone home on their mobile to say they've arrived, check their phone for messages half an hour later, phone the next day to see if the cat has had its dinner, check for messages, and phone again on Sunday to tell their family they are coming home soon. The mobile phone revolution has made possible much that is useful: phoning ahead if you're going to be late for a meeting, or texting a relative the other side of the world. But it also gives rise to all sorts of calls and worries that wouldn't have even occurred to us before.

Sometimes, rather than using technology, technology starts to use us. Or rather, the technology becomes a way in which we distract ourselves from experiencing our own hearts and minds.

So perhaps simplicity involves asking ourselves what is really necessary for pursuing our true purpose, and for that dwelling in possibility. We ask ourselves what activities or possessions help us to do this, and which detract from it. We ask the same question at work. Perhaps, as we pursue spiritual practice, our work becomes, in certain ways, less central in our lives. Our sense of worth, or self-image, becomes less dependent on our job and status. Perhaps we do not see promotion, high earnings, and career success as all-important as it once might have been. We know there are other aspects to our lives that are we value more highly, and deeper and more vital currents that run through us.

exercise – *my work as right livelihood?*

You might like to go back over the four elements of right livelihood we have discussed, and consider the strengths and weaknesses of your work or life-activity under each of the four headings.

Give this reflection adequate time – allowing at least twenty minutes – so there is scope for your observations and thoughts to emerge gradually. It is also good to make a few notes as you go.

Then look back at what you have written. Are there areas of your work you are especially happy with? Are there areas you would like to develop? What resources would you need, or what changes would you need to make, in order to do this?

Everyone will have a different way of combining these four elements of right livelihood. These are not hard and fast rules; what is best for one person isn't necessarily best for another. One person may decline promotion because they know it will entail staying late to deal with the increased responsibilities, and they want that time to meditate; another will seek promotion because they feel they need the challenge and the chance to make a bigger contribution in their organization. One person might be able to live very simply on little money; another might want to earn more because they've been used to a higher standard of living all their life. One person might work as little as possible because they are pursuing other interests: a book they are writing, voluntary work, or a study group. Another might be working long hours, but be totally and healthily engaged in their work: it is their medium for developing themselves and making a contribution to the world.

It is our choice. We have to make our own path, and find a way that works for us. We can, however, get the help, advice, or inspiration from others on the path. At the Buddhist centre where I work, there have been, at various times, groups of people who've met up to talk about their way of practising. There has been a parents group, and a group for social workers, for example. Having people practising in different ways is healthy. Everyone has their own contribution to make. Overall, it creates a rich mix and allows us to see spiritual ideals expressed in a variety of ways. This can help prevent us confusing the expression of an ideal with the ideal itself.

One friend of mine, after he had been meditating for a few years, trained to become a teacher. He has been a happy and successful primary school teacher for some years now, and you can see the positive effect it has had on him. He also says that his work has changed him as much as meditation, but that he couldn't have made the change to his work without meditation. His is an example of a life of activity and a life of calm working together.

buddhism in the west

Buddhism originated with the Buddha's experience of Enlightenment 2,500 years ago in north-east India. Since then, it has spread over much of the world and helped others taste this Enlightenment for themselves. Wherever it has gone, Buddhism has adapted itself. In order to be understood, it has adopted the language and culture of the people it meets. To remain relevant and practicable, it has developed new forms of organization and practice.

More recently, Buddhism has encountered western society. If Buddhism is to take hold here, it will need to undergo another transformation. The same message of freedom will have to be translated into our culture. New ways of practice suitable for that culture will gradually evolve through experiment and accumulated experience.

In the East, it was often the monks that did most spiritual practice: it was they who meditated and studied the texts. The lay people supported the monks financially, performed rituals at the temple, and tried to lead ethical lives, but they did not necessarily meditate or study Buddhist teachings. This might be a surprise to us. However, in traditional societies reading and writing was the preserve of the few and leisure time was short. This meant that intense, committed spiritual practice also necessarily became the preserve of an élite. (You can see the same pattern in the history of Christianity.)

But in today's society, the vast majority can read and gain access to literature, and there is more leisure time available, so a different pattern of practice can emerge. Although it is still very early days, there is perhaps such a pattern emerging in Western Buddhism. Most people practising Buddhism in the West are doing so as lay people, but they are seriously committed practitioners who meditate and go on retreat.

If, wherever Buddhism has flowered anew, it has made a further contribution to the overall tradition, then perhaps the special contribution of Western Buddhism will be the development of right livelihood. It would be a wonderful thing if Buddhist ethical ideals and methods (such as those for developing awareness) could make a significant impact on Western society and economic life.

But there are, as always, dangers too. In this process of translation we need to ensure that we are adapting Buddhism to address our situation, and not watering it down or getting it out of balance. Perhaps, if a characteristic of Western Buddhism is that it is practice in the world, we need to ensure that there are some who also, from time to time, step away from the world, immerse themselves in meditation, and then return to reinspire and renew the practice of all.

6

daily life

coursing the worldly winds

Man was made for Joy & Woe;
And when this we rightly know
Thro' the World we safely go.
Joy & Woe are woven fine,
A Clothing for the soul Divine;
Under every grief & pine
Runs a joy with silken twine.[19]

The previous chapter was concerned with how to take our practice into everyday life, but in some ways the approach was rather theoretical. We were looking in principle at the idea of 'practice in the world'. This chapter will try to convey more of the nuts and bolts of such a practice, and an actual, lived sense of what it might entail. We will do this through an exploration of what are known as the 'worldly winds'.

The eight worldly winds (or *lokadhammas*, as they are called in the early Buddhist tradition) are arranged in a series of four pairs: gain and loss, fame and infamy, praise and blame, and pleasure and pain. These will give us a framework for looking at some of the twists and turns of the path, the various challenges that can suddenly be thrown at us, and towards which we can try to respond with more awareness and loving-kindness. Some of these challenges will just be small and everyday; others may be of greater significance in our story. The teaching of the worldly winds is designed to help us see and dwell in the possibility afforded by these challenges – to see such situations as opportunities to learn and grow.

The worldly winds are fluctuating conditions that just 'blow about' in the world. Although we can do our best to influence the world and make it go the way we want, we can't control things completely. The world is too big and complex. No matter how well we live our lives, there will be factors over which we have no control. These ups and downs of life will arise when we least expect them. The worldly winds may be blowing gently one day; the next day a gale may be howling in the opposite direction. Today life is a breeze and everything goes brilliantly; tomorrow it seems that nothing goes right and we wish we'd not bothered getting out of bed. Sometimes we get what we want, people praise us, and life is enjoyable. But at other times, we lose things we really like, we don't seem to be popular, and life is painful.

When we experience gain, fame, praise, or pleasure we can often feel elated, our sense of self-worth increases, we feel more confident and in charge of our lives. But loss, infamy, blame, or pain can cause us to feel despondent, our sense of self-worth diminishes, our confidence decreases, and we can lose initiative. We can feel a victim of circumstance.

The Buddhist teaching of the worldly winds helps us to be more aware of these forces and their effect upon us. First, we'll explore each pair in turn in order to see exactly what it is they are describing and whether we recognize them within our own lives. With more awareness of them, we can navigate them more skilfully. Secondly, we'll consider how we might respond to the worldly winds when they arise.

Most of the following examples will be small and everyday ones. This may leave you wondering about the more difficult times, when we experience loss or pain, such as bereavement or serious illness. We're deliberately looking at the smaller occurrences first, precisely because these are the easiest to work with, and they are the ones that are cropping up day by day. At the end of this chapter, we will look briefly at those times in our lives when the worldly winds are blowing more strongly, times of more extreme difficulty. There are, of course, no glib or easy answers to these challenges, but let us hope we will still find that the teaching of the worldly winds can help us orientate ourselves in the midst of the storm.

gain and loss

These worldly winds are at work when we are blown about by the gain or loss of anything at all, be it possessions, people, role or position, or health. We can experience gain or loss driving in traffic. Either the traffic lights stay green as we approach, or a car in front of us is slow and they turn red. Someone pushes in front of us, or they give way to let us out at a busy junction. We get stuck in a long queue of vehicles, or we choose the best lane of traffic and go sailing past everyone else in the queue.

Someone we really value in our organization, and whom it would be hard to replace, decides to leave and we experience loss. Or they decide to stay and we experience gain. We are queuing in a shop and someone pushes in – we may have an experience of loss. I've been interested to watch my response in this kind of situation. Part of what goes on in me is that my pride is hurt. I find myself hoping that no one else noticed their getting one over on me. In other words, it is loss of face that has annoyed me, as much as losing my place in the queue.

We are shopping and we find exactly the shirt we want, at a bargain price: gain. We discover that someone has just got the last one in our size: loss. Watching our secret, inner response can be revealing. Are we annoyed and jealous? I often experience gain and loss in respect of time: I'm engaged with a task and think I've got plenty of time. I'm sure there will be enough left at the end of the day to do something that I enjoy. But then the job takes longer than expected and I find myself rushing to get it done. I can feel disgruntlement and a sense of loss of the time I thought I had.

fame and infamy

Fame and infamy are rather strong words, suggesting popularity or notoriety on a large scale. We live in a celebrity-obsessed culture in which it seems that some people will do almost anything to remain in the public eye, or in which politicians and public figures can suddenly fall from favour and find themselves vilified by the media. But, in smaller ways, and within our own social circle, when we notice our own equanimity disturbed by whether we are popular or well liked, or whether we are the centre of attention, then the worldly winds of fame and infamy are blowing.

It is natural to want to be popular, appreciated, and noticed by others. But if we find ourselves laughing at jokes, or agreeing with opinions, just in order to fit in and be liked, then we are giving way to these worldly winds. Or we don't speak out and express our opinion in a meeting, because we fear disapproval. We shouldn't underestimate the strength of the desire to be liked in this way; it is very strong, almost instinctual. It can be extremely difficult to stand up against a group of people.

Perhaps we observe ourselves jostling for attention and prominence. Conversations can sometimes become competitions – the participants hardly waiting for the last person to finish speaking before they are jumping in with a joke or anecdote that trumps what has just been said.

When I teach a Buddhist class, or give a talk, it sometimes goes well, but then at other times I'm not quite on form, and it isn't so well received. Afterwards, I can notice an underlying feeling of elation or dejection – the signs that the worldly winds of fame and infamy are holding sway.

praise and blame

Whereas we might experience fame and infamy with regard to our general reputation and prominence among others, the worldly winds of praise and blame are experienced with regard to how specific things we have *done*, or actions we have taken, are seen by others. Sometimes people like what we've done, and they approve and give praise. At other times, our actions are disapproved of, and we encounter blame or criticism.

Your sales team at work exceeds its monthly target, and the management is happy: praise. Or several members of the team are off sick, you fall short of your target, the managers want to know what's happened: blame.

These worldly winds are inevitable. Our actions will not suit everyone all the time. Sometimes the same action will elicit both praise and blame. We recently redecorated the shrine room in our Buddhist centre. We painted the walls a bold, deep red, and the ceiling dark blue with gold stars. We had some strong responses! Some people praised the design. One woman walked in and liked it so much she gave us a donation towards the costs on the spot. But of course it was not to everyone's taste, and some people criticized it. If we had tried to find a colour that everyone liked, the walls would have stayed unpainted for a very long time! But when one has a personal investment in something, it is hard not to be over-sensitive to the worldly winds of praise and blame.

Sometimes we are blamed for something that we were responsible for, at other times we might receive it unjustly. If we are in a position of responsibility, we sometimes have to take the rap for something that we weren't directly involved in. For instance, you find yourself on the receiving end of an angry customer who received shoddy service from another member of staff. You weren't even at work that day. This just comes with the territory. We should try not to look for someone else to blame, or feel resentful and sorry for ourselves.

pleasure and pain

Sometimes life is pleasurable, sometimes it brings us pain. One day, all of us will face serious illness or old age. These worldly winds are, like the others, universal. But there are smaller, everyday instances too. All of us suffer physically from time to time: a toothache, headache, a sprained muscle. In the staff room we've run out of milk again. At home, just as we get the first really cold weather of the year, the heating breaks down. In the summer there's a heat wave: at weekends it is glorious, but commuting to work, and in the office, it is hell.

How blown about are we by these small, everyday occurrences of pleasure and pain? Do we feel irritated when the milk runs out, or do we just try our tea black? How well can we maintain our equanimity when the weather conditions are unpleasant?

exercise – *recognizing the worldly winds*

As with all the reflections in this book, give this exercise plenty of time, a quiet space in which to do it, and take notes as you go.

Go back over each of the four pairs of worldly winds and think of as many instances as you can when they blow you about and you lose equanimity. Take into account both sides of each pair, e.g. how you are affected by gain, as well as by loss.

Are you more affected by some winds than by others? Do you have a particular susceptibility to one of them? Or are there even other factors that blow you around that aren't quite covered by the traditional list? (A friend of mine came up with success and failure; he realized he was quite vulnerable to fear of failure and desire for success.)

practising awareness and acceptance

If, as we saw in Chapter 1, impermanence and change are basic facts of life, then the conditions of our lives will constantly change too. The world is vast and complex, so many different conditions and influences are at play. How can we expect them constantly to arrange themselves according to what we want? In a way, we could view the times when life does work as a miracle, rather than seeing it as a surprising and infuriating injustice when it doesn't. Although we can always have an influence on the world and what life deals us, we cannot control it. When the worldly winds blow, we just have to learn to navigate through them as safely we can. The ups and downs of life cannot be avoided, but they can be responded to with more or less awareness and creativity. But this is not always easy: the winds blow around us, they stir up waves that toss us about, and we can lose our bearings.

So acknowledging the worldly winds does not mean being passive towards the world, drifting wherever the winds blow us, and ignoring our real needs. In some circumstances it is fine to want certain results and strive towards them. The trouble comes when we refuse to accept things not going our way, because there is so much emotion invested in a particular outcome. But if we can hold events in a wider perspective and not be so set on getting exactly what we want, we will have a more even experience of life.

We can see three aspects to navigating the worldly winds. First, there is awareness that they are there and that they affect us. If we bear the four pairs in mind in our daily life, we may start noticing more and more ways in which they influence us.

Secondly, we can try to practise acceptance. If we cannot change what is happening, we just have to let go and accept what is. We can start with small things, and even this can be surprisingly difficult. Sometimes, when the milk has run out, I catch myself looking through every cupboard in the kitchen just to check there isn't a spare carton somewhere. On some level, I'm emotionally unable to accept even a small thing like running out of milk! I just don't want it to be true!

I once worked in a team of people who had just taken over running a small publishing business. None of us had any experience of publishing, so those first few months saw us thrown well and truly in at the deep end. There was one member of the team who, when things went wrong and nerves were likely to get fraught, would choose exactly that time to wander off to the café. This used to frustrate me – how could they be so irresponsible? But then I realized that what they were doing was, in a way, stepping back from the situation so that they could see it more clearly and accept it for what it was. Then they could be clearer about how best to respond to the situation. This was far better than remaining in the office, rushing around like a headless chicken and hoping the problem would go away. We need to breathe deeply and try to relax into the situations we find ourselves in. Only if we can be aware of the worldly winds and practise some acceptance of our circumstances, can we start bringing a new quality into play.

Thirdly, we can start dwelling in possibility, rather than denying reality. I suggest, below, some of the qualities we might practise. Rather than being tossed about by the worldly winds, we introduce a new factor that raises us above the situation. The quality I've suggested in each case is my own idea, not from a traditional teaching. It is also merely one possible suggestion; there may well be other qualities that would also steer us safely through the winds and stormy waters.

from gain and loss into generosity

As a way of keeping a sense of equanimity between the worldly winds of gain and loss, we could focus on the quality of generosity. Instead of relating to the world in terms of what we can get, we may attempt to relate to it in terms of what we can give. For example, we could try to be generous in busy traffic. If we let a few people out at a junction, it will make hardly any difference to our journey time, but we (and they) will arrive home in a better frame of mind. We might find that we don't need things as much as we thought. If someone else got that bargain shirt – well, we could be glad for him or her.

As we adopt this attitude, we may find ourselves loosening our hold on all sorts of things. We might become less controlling and more flexible, less possessive of things and people. Most importantly, we will start to feel more at ease in ourselves.

from fame and infamy into integrity

If we notice ourselves being blown about by the worldly winds of fame and infamy, we could try to practise integrity. This word indicates a kind of wholeness, or honesty. When we possess integrity, we can stand by our own values, beliefs, and opinions, while also being willing to change them if we see a better way. But we wouldn't change merely for the sake of popularity or to fit in with others. It is only by sticking to our opinions that we are able to learn, refine, and adapt them. If we bend and give way at the slightest opposition, our beliefs are never tested.

Maybe we get upset because we realize we are not liked by a number of people at work. But we will never be popular with everyone. Especially if we have responsibility, or have to make decisions that affect others, there are always going to be some people who like us, and others whom we rub up the wrong way. We mustn't be too worried about this. There isn't necessarily anything wrong with us just because someone doesn't like us. It is not that we shouldn't care what they think, but we don't need to be overly concerned either. I used to be far too concerned about upsetting people with my opinions. I eventually realized that if I said something that I believed, with good intentions, this was all I could do. The other person's response was their own choice. Sometimes we can be overly responsible for other people in this way – because we want to be liked.

So we try to practise integrity and honesty, speaking out for what we value and feel is right, but not needing to be the centre of attention, or to have everyone always agree with our point of view. And we try to maintain realistic expectations – knowing that we'll never be constantly popular with everyone. We will be unpopular at times, especially if we have strong beliefs and ideas. Sometimes we just have to endure the discomfort this brings, and practise integrity.

There is another story about Hakuin, the Zen teacher we met in the previous chapter. In the village where he once lived, a girl became pregnant by a local farmer's boy. To protect the boy, the girl claimed that Hakuin was the father of the child. Her parents were furious and angrily denounced him. Hakuin could see that he would only be thought more guilty if he protested his innocence, so he simply said, 'Is that so?' Of course, for a monk to get a young girl pregnant was a real disgrace – and probably the whole village would have been outraged. When the child was born it was given to Hakuin to look after.

After a while the girl could no longer hide the truth and she told her parents what had really happened. They went to Hakuin and offered their apologies. He handed back the child, saying simply, 'Is that so?'

Hakuin demonstrated great integrity, in the sense of a lack of concern for his reputation. He just did the right thing in the circumstances – willing to look after the child and equally willing to give it up again – regardless of what others thought of him. However, we needn't take the story literally. If we are unjustly accused, there is nothing wrong with pointing out the truth and defending our reputation. On the contrary, clearly speaking the truth may well be the right thing to do.

from praise and blame into appreciation

When on the receiving end of blame, we don't want to accept it. We tell ourselves that life is not fair. But the idea that fairness is always possible is a myth (which is not to say we shouldn't try to make life as fair as it can be). However, one antidote to the choppy waters created by the winds of praise and blame might be *appreciation*.

First, we try to appreciate ourselves and our own efforts. We reflect that we're not perfect, but we are doing the best we can.

We can also try to appreciate other people. We try to create a culture of appreciation, rather than a culture of blame. For example, when circumstances are difficult and people are on edge, the culture in a workplace or organization can become overly critical. Blaming and fault-finding abound. But if we can engender a spirit of appreciation of people's efforts, realize that they too are probably doing their best, the atmosphere will lighten and everyone will feel less stressed.

In addition, if we do recognize each other's achievements and efforts in this way, we will probably find that we are all more able to give and receive genuine and constructive criticism. If the overall ethos is one of appreciation, we are more likely to be able to admit when we have made a mistake, and want to learn to do better.

from pleasure and pain into contentment

What is pleasure? You could argue that much of the pleasure inherent in something is simply the release of the craving you had for it, rather than a quality of the thing itself. If we're given just a glass of water to drink, we're sometimes a bit disappointed. But after a hard morning's work in the hot sun, that cool, refreshing water is just what we want. Receiving the same object can be the occasion of pleasure or pain in different circumstances. When we were hoping for wine or fruit juice, the water doesn't satisfy our craving and we can't enjoy it. But when we're desperate for a drink, the water does slake our thirst and we feel pleasure. So, perhaps pleasure, or happiness, is actually the *absence* of craving, rather than the *presence* of a particular desired object. Happiness is a state of being content and free from desire. Conversely, displeasure is a state of wanting something to stop or to go away. We crave its cessation. But if we can just accept it and let that craving go, then our experience of the thing itself is not nearly as bad.

The Buddha once spoke about this using the simile of an archer firing two arrows at us. The first is the arrow of a physical pain. But we then let the archer fire a second arrow – that of mental pain. On top of the physical discomfort we add layers of mental pain by resisting, resenting, and wishing the physical pain would go away. In so doing, we make the pain worse than it has to be. We sometimes make it even worse for ourselves by adding on the pain of irritation or impatience, with that inner voice saying, 'It's not fair, why is this happening to me?' The Buddha is suggesting that, even when we cannot remove the first arrow, we can at least remove the second. Sometimes we can just be aware of an unpleasant experience – and find it is not as bad as we imagined. Rather than pushing it away, we let the experience be there. We practise awareness and acceptance – which may lead to some measure of contentment, despite the discomfort.

So to help us deal with the worldly winds of pleasure and pain, we can try cultivating contentment. We can do this by enjoying what is pleasurable in our lives and really appreciating it, looking to ensure there is time and space in our routine for beauty and aliveness. We can refine our pleasures and look for things and activities that will give us more inner contentment. We try to ensure there is at least some time for such activities – a walk in the countryside, or a wander round the garden. We can reward ourselves with something we know we will enjoy if we have been working hard or facing a difficult time.

exercise – *finding your own antidotes*

Go back to the first exercise and the notes you made on how the worldly winds affect you. Consider whether there are new qualities that you could try bringing into the situations you listed in that exercise. You can make use of my suggestions, or think of your own, as appropriate.

Again, do this for each of the four pairs of worldly winds.

Choose one, and try to put it into practice for a week. How do you get on? Is it easy to remember when you're in the thick of it? Do you find it makes a difference?

You could return to other pairs and work with them in subsequent weeks.

coursing the worldly winds

You may be thinking this is all right as far as relatively minor examples, such as a toothache or a traffic jam, go, but what about more serious situations in which the worldly winds blow? What about losing our job so that we can't pay our mortgage, or dealing with the pain of serious illness or injury?

In a way, a lot of the examples given in this chapter *are* pretty trivial. But they are the kinds of issues that crop up every day. And, although they are only minor, if we are honest, do we have to admit that they still blow us about? Can we still feel life is unfair to us, and feel irritated and resentful? In other words, even working with these small, but frequent, instances of the worldly winds could make a big difference to the quality of our lives.

We can also regard our working creatively with the small occurrences as helping us prepare for the bigger ones. Of course, we hope that we experience the real hardships of life as little as possible, but they will come to all of us at some point. At such a time, we will be really glad of any ability we have acquired to respond with creativity, possibility, and openness. If we are well practised at coursing the worldly winds when they are only gusty, and the waters merely choppy, we will be more prepared for when they are blowing a full gale and the waves are huge. If we are used to being aware of when we lose our equanimity, and of trying to bring in a new quality to raise us above the choppy waters, then we will be better trained for when the big storms come.

Not that we should expect ourselves to manage perfectly, but we will be more used to navigating difficult waters than we might have otherwise have been.

As we learn to course the worldly winds, we are learning to take them less personally. We see that they are just part of the ebb and flow of life. We realize that they come and go; none of them will last for ever. This is true of those we experience as positive, such as gain and praise. But it is also true for those we experience as negative, such as loss and pain. And realizing they are just part of life, we understand that they happen to everyone. It isn't that life is necessarily treating us worse than anyone else. Some people have experienced calmer, more pleasant breezes than us, but others will have experienced much more of a storm.

However much we practise, we will still be subject to the worldly winds. But we don't have to be so affected by them, so thrown off course by despondency or loss of confidence. We can pick ourselves up and carry on. To change the metaphor somewhat, imagine a big ship in a stormy sea. The waves just wash up against the sides of the ship and it hardly sways at all. It stays firmly on course. A little boat, however, is thrown about by even the smallest waves. Our practice – especially that of loving-kindness – makes us, in a sense, bigger and more robust.

The worldly winds will always be present. But if they affect us less severely, we will have a positive effect on others. If we are able to remain calm and steady, it helps others to do so too. Perhaps we can tie smaller boats behind us and help pull them to calmer waters.

Eventually, there does come a point when we see through the worldly winds and they cannot touch us at all. We have understood their nature and realize they are just air – empty – there is nothing really there at all. But that is for a later chapter.

7

friendship
talking about mysteries

I have always loved friends of the way,
Always held them dear.
Meeting a stranger with silent springs,
Greeting a guest talking truth,
Talking about mysteries on a moonlit night,
Searching for truth until dawn.
When the tracks of our inventions disappear,
And we see who we really are.[20]

Perhaps you've been attending a Buddhist meditation group for some months and you begin to notice certain things. Do you often find that the best meditation of your week happens when you are meditating with other people? Perhaps it is hard to meditate at all when you are on our own, but sitting quietly with a number of people, and with the meditation being led, your mind becomes quieter and more still. Is it your experience that there is an atmosphere in the group that is conducive to deeper concentration?

You might notice other tendencies. For example, the wish to discuss something that happened in your meditation, or get other people's views on an ethical dilemma, or ask questions to clarify something you read. We may find that within a group of people who are exploring Buddhism and meditation together, you can talk about these things in a way that other people might not quite understand or relate to. While non-Buddhist friends may respect your ideals, you will find much more of a resonance among those treading the same path. You might find these discussions very helpful, even inspiring.

In other words, we sense that we have a lot to gain by practising, and sharing our experience, with other people who are also practising. This is what is known in Buddhism as *sangha* – which means 'spiritual community'.

In a previous chapter we looked at some of the supports that are necessary to our practice of Buddhism. These supports are crucial, especially if we are practising in the context of a busy life 'in the world'. We have already looked at meditation, retreats, and right livelihood. In this chapter we will be suggesting that spiritual community – a group of people who are meditating, studying Buddhist teachings, and exploring the spiritual life together – is another such support. Later, we'll ask how you might find a sangha if you are not already in touch with one. But first we'll look more at why it is important, and what sangha can provide.

we are all interconnected

I recently took part in an exercise in which, in our imagination, we went back to our childhood and reflected on our earliest relationships – those with our parents and siblings. We were asked to consider how we were in those relationships, in particular whether there was a part of ourselves we left out, or some way we learned to behave, in order to keep the relationships stable and harmonious (at least on the surface). In other words, did we make a kind of unspoken contract in order to keep the peace?

We followed that up by reflecting on subsequent episodes in our lives, and how we unconsciously continued obeying that contract in our relationships with other people. Most of us doing the exercise could see a pattern that had played itself out, again and again, all the way through our lives. Perhaps we had been unable to talk about certain emotions early on in life, and we could see how we had carried on like this in many relationships throughout our lives. Even that very day, we could still see the patterns influencing how we participated in the workshop.

One thing the exercise demonstrated is how strong an influence we can have on each other. The parent–child influence is probably particularly strong, but we all influence each other in a myriad ways, each and every day. In conscious or unconscious ways, obvious or subtle, we are influenced by the ideas, moods, behaviour, and attitudes of people around us. We, likewise, are having an effect on them.

exercise – *influences*

Spend some time reflecting on people who've had a positive influence on you. Slowly think through your life-story and jot down influential people as they occur to you.

These might be people who've been close to you, or those with whom you had a fleeting, but significant, contact. They might be people you've not actually met: the author of a book that had a profound impact on you, or a public figure or famous personality. Some of the influences may have been dramatic and instantly life-changing, others may have been quieter and less obvious.

If you give this exercise long enough, you may even start recalling influences that you've not previously considered, or not thought about for a long time.

A sangha is a group of people who get together because they want to help influence each other in the direction of spiritual freedom, or Enlightenment. This is where we can encourage each other to dwell in possibility, try to help each other become more creative with our lives, wanting each person to be at their very best.

As we noticed earlier, even when a group of people meditate together, we can get a sense of this interconnectedness and mutual influence that is sangha. When we meditate with others, a quiet and peaceful atmosphere can arise, one that is supportive to each individual's personal practice. Although no one else can do our mediation for us, we can help and influence each other by creating that meditative ambience together. (This might even be an inspiring way to approach the weekly meditation with your group: to see it as something you are doing to support each other's efforts and aspirations, not just for your individual benefit.)

We can have an 'enlightening' influence on each other in other ways too. If we want to find out more about how to put Buddhism into practice, there may be people at the class with the experience and knowledge to help us do this. At other times, we may have something to contribute from our own knowledge and experience. We can discuss issues, problems, and questions that arise out of our attempts to practise, and bring the collective wisdom and experience of the group to bear on them. We find that we can be ourselves – and our ideals and aspirations will be understood, taken seriously, and respected. This gives us more confidence to take our ideals seriously. For some people it can even be a deep relief to find others who think and feel as they do.

It is sometimes said that the spiritual life is 'caught, not taught'. We cannot really learn about a quality such as kindness or confidence by reading about it in a book, although that may help to some extent. We usually need to see it exemplified. We need a more tangible sense of what it would be like by seeing that quality in someone else. It is not that we then want to mimic them. We cannot be them, we have to be ourselves, but we can get sparked off, or be inspired, by seeing others practising. They may not have the quality perfectly, but it is almost all the more inspiring for that. You see how someone else has had to struggle and work to change old habits. In other words, it is not the perfection of that quality that they are exemplifying, but the *process* of perfection and the striving.

four qualities of sangha

The poem at the start of this chapter is by Han Shan, a Chinese Buddhist poet whom scholars believe lived in the late eighth and early ninth centuries. To me, the poem's eight lines can be divided into four pairs, each pair having something to say about the qualities we should find in sangha: there should be friendship, an ethos that is open and welcoming, mutual exploration of the truth, and authenticity.

First, Han Shan says he loves his 'friends of the way', and 'always held them dear'. If we are to help each other on the spiritual path, there must be an atmosphere of friendship and loving-kindness. In the Buddhist tradition there is a beautiful expression, *kalyana mitrata*. *Kalyana* means 'lovely or good', and *mitrata* is 'friendship'. The term is often translated as 'spiritual friendship' or 'friendship based on the good'. Real friendship sees the good, or the potential good, in someone and brings that out more fully. We see someone's good qualities and also their weaknesses. We can hold both sides of them in awareness, while loving them and wanting their happiness. We can love someone despite their faults, because we see through the faults to their true potential.

There is a famous incident in the life of the Buddha in which Ananda, the Buddha's cousin and oldest friend, remarks that spiritual friendship is half the spiritual life. The Buddha interjects and says that it is not. It is, he says, the *whole* of the spiritual life. It is interesting to reflect that the Buddha puts it as strongly as that.

Deep friendship does not develop overnight. It may take many years to mature. Nevertheless, right from the start, sangha is characterized to some extent by friendliness and appreciation.

In the second two lines of the poem, Han Shan meets strangers and greets guests. In other words, a sangha aims to be open, accessible, and expansive. It is not a closed group that doesn't allow anyone else to join. Spiritual community is not just about our getting the support we need for our practice. It is also about helping others gain support for their practice.

In our weekly group, we might help with ordinary practical things, like making the tea. This may seem a very small thing, but it helps create a harmony between us. In a discussion, we participate as best we can, maybe offering a perspective, or an experience we've had, that others might find helpful. Or we just ask the odd question. This can also be a valuable contribution. We are friendly towards people who are new to the group and make them feel welcome. We realize that sangha is not a commodity that we acquire, but an ethos that is created between us.

When we do any of these things to help create an environment beneficial to others, we can learn much ourselves. For example, to explain an idea or practice to other people, you need to be clear about your own understanding and experience. It requires constant reflection, which helps keep the teachings fresh and alive for you, too. It is harder to settle down into assumptions and fixed understandings of things, because you have been stimulated to think anew. In this way, spiritual community becomes not only a support for self-development, but a means of spiritual transformation in its own right.

Next, we find Han Shan 'talking about mysteries on a moonlit night, searching for truth until dawn.' The moon is often symbolic of wisdom, and these lines evoke a sense of wonder, discovery, and mutual exploration of the questions and paradoxes of life. Perhaps sangha should have something of this flavour, too. We are able to explore together the deepest questions, to delve into the mysteries of existence. Perhaps it would be too much to expect this every week, but occasionally we touch on something profound and real, and there is that air of excitement and discovery.

Finally, 'the tracks of our inventions disappear, and we see who we really are.' Through an atmosphere of love, openness, and mutual exploration, the barriers between us come down. We can thus be ourselves more and more fully. We don't, any longer, through insecurity and fear of rejection, have to keep up the pretence, or leave out certain aspects of ourselves out in our interactions with others. When this happens, it can be an immense relief. It can allow us to really change and let go of old patterns of behaviour.

When you see people in a positive environment, where they are loved and appreciated, you do sometimes notice the 'tracks of invention' gradually disappear, and they can become more truly themselves. The genuine, individual person glows more brightly and clearly. Spiritual growth sometimes seems to involve peeling off old layers so that the real person, with all their qualities, can shine forth.

So spiritual community needs to encourage us to be more ourselves, more individual, more authentic – even more eccentric, if that's what we truly are. Human groups have a tendency to encourage conformity, because this helps keep the group cohesive, albeit on a superficial level. This tendency is also present in a sangha, but a spiritual community at its best will engender an atmosphere in which we can encourage one another to be more truly ourselves. If it is really sangha, it will have this flavour of authentic, honest communication – at least to some extent. Hence it will also have a genuine sense of diversity.

But although there is individuality and authenticity, within a sangha we will also find harmony. We may all be different, but we relate on the basis of shared ideals. Where there are common ideals, it is possible to disagree strongly on some issues, and to debate animatedly. We are able to do so because, deeper down, there are understandings that *are* shared, and a basic trust of people's intentions.

An obvious analogy for this combination of individuality and harmony is an orchestra: each musician plays their own instrument and their part of the music, but does so with an awareness of all the others, so that together they play music that is truly wonderful, in which the whole is greater than sum of its parts, much richer and fuller than anything they could have played on their own.

how to find a sangha

How can we find a sangha? These days, we are lucky in that there are quite a few different Buddhist traditions established in many places in the West. We can try these out and see what suits us. There are Theravada, Tibetan, Zen, and Western Buddhist groups. There is not space here to do justice to the richness of each of these traditions, but they have each evolved in a different culture in order to meet the spiritual needs of certain people. So while they will have much in common, they will each have a distinctive flavour and approach.

If there isn't a group near you, it may be that you can occasionally travel to visit a retreat centre. Or perhaps you could have contact with other practitioners via the Internet. You might even think about starting a meditation group of your own – gathering a few people to meditate together and occasionally inviting a Buddhist teacher or speaker.

In this chapter, we've looked in some detail at the benefits and qualities of spiritual community, but in the end it is something to be experienced, not just talked about. It is, in this respect, like meditation. While it is helpful to talk about it at first, you then have to try it for yourself and make up your own mind. Only when it is lived and experienced can you draw your own conclusions.

In a way, we have been talking about spiritual community in a rather idealized manner. It will not always be like this. A lot of the time, our communication may be rather humdrum and ordinary. Perhaps we are not able to fire each other up every time we meet! In any group there will sometimes be awkward dynamics and people who don't fit in easily. It may even be you who finds it hard to fit in – perhaps you find groups difficult and have to learn to work with that. Whoever we meet in a sangha, there will be some people we are naturally drawn to, and others who we are not so attracted to. Maybe they even irritate us. All this is part of the practice of sangha – trying to understand others more deeply, develop kindness, and relate to the best in people.

Whatever sangha you find, it won't be perfect. It is guaranteed that the people there won't act with perfect wisdom and compassion all the time. They will be like you: ordinary human beings doing their best on the path. If you read about the sangha of the Buddha's time, you'll discover it was just the same. There was once a heated dispute that threatened to split the whole sangha. It started, incredible (or laughable) though it may seem, with a trivial incident in which a monk left a jar of unused water in the latrine, and another monk found it there. This was against their rules of etiquette, so it developed into a full-blown argument with rumours, accusations, and monks from miles around taking sides. The Buddha tried to reason with the monks, but when he saw he was getting nowhere he simply walked off into the forest to get away from it all. It was some weeks before the monks noticed the Buddha was staying away, whereupon they decided to mend their ways.[21]

But although sangha will not be perfect, we can hope that there will at least be an open, friendly atmosphere, clear instructions and teachings, and a spirit of freedom and authenticity. If these are present, sangha can be of tremendous benefit.[22]

exercise – *our experience of sangha*

If you are new to a Buddhist group, you might find it too early to answer these questions meaningfully. On the other hand, you might find they throw up some useful ideas and reflections.

With a pencil and paper, a quiet space, and sufficient time, jot down responses to the following.

Are you drawn to being part of a sangha? Or is it something you are wary of, or resistant to? If so, why is this?

What is your experience of sangha so far? Are there benefits you have noticed, or things that make you uncomfortable? Referring back to Han Shan's qualities of sangha, is there an element you would like to experience more of? Is there a way in which you could contribute more?

teachers and disciples

In traditional Buddhism there is an emphasis on finding a teacher with whom we can have a one-to-one relationship, and who guides us on the path. Different traditions see the nature of this relationship in various ways. In the early traditions, for example, the teacher is an experienced practitioner who is able to hand on their knowledge, and provide the necessary instruction. In the Tibetan traditions, however, the teacher is the *guru*: he or she is actually the Buddha, as far as the student is concerned. They play the role of the Buddha in that they provide the teachings that can lead to liberation. So profound gratitude and reverence towards them is encouraged.

However, in the West, the cultural context is rather different. For a start, when we first attend a group we may not be looking for a teacher at all. We just want to learn how to meditate and find out a bit about Buddhism. How, then, do we relate to the person leading our Buddhist group? In addition, on the shrine at our Buddhist centre there might be a picture of a founding figure or important teacher. Does this mean that everyone is supposed to have an attitude of reverence towards this person?

The important thing is not to feel that you have to relate to them in any particular way. We should, of course, be respectful of people, but anything beyond this is up to us. Some people who have been involved at our centre may naturally feel a strong sense of gratitude to the person in the photograph for founding their sangha, but it would be unreasonable to expect everyone to feel this way towards someone they hardly know, or may never have met.

The teacher-disciple relationship has been a source of difficulty as Buddhism has evolved in Western society. There are many stories of disciples being disappointed, angry, or disillusioned with the whole spiritual path once they discover that the teacher they had looked up to has behaved unwisely or unskilfully.

It seems there is something in the ethics of our culture that encourages us to view people in a very black-and-white way. Either they are wonderful and up on a shiny pedestal, or they are terrible and come crashing to earth. There is no in-between. However, we need to have a realistic view of people, recognizing and valuing their good qualities, but also being aware that they will have weaknesses. Some Western practitioners, taught by teachers who were later caught up in controversy, will say that although their teacher has behaved in ways they cannot explain or condone, they still gave them something that no one else could give them – the precious gift of the path to freedom. For that, they are deeply grateful. In the East, people seem naturally to be able to see their teachers in this way, but in the West this understanding has sometimes been harder won.

These difficulties arise partly out of a natural, human tendency to project. Because the values and ideals we encounter through the person that is teaching or leading our group are so important to us, we see them as somehow embodying them. We project those qualities onto them, and consequently see them in rather an idealized way. As we have seen, this can lead to pain and disappointment if we later discover they were not as perfect as we thought. It can also be painful for them too. When someone is projecting either positive or negative qualities onto you, the artificiality of this can be felt quite tangibly.

On the other hand, there is no need to be frightened of this area. We don't want to go to the other extreme – always having a sceptical view of people and assuming they must have some terrible dark side they are hiding. In other words, we just try to relate to people in a natural, human way, appreciating what may well be impressive about them, but also retaining a sense of perspective.

Over time, friendships will develop in our own particular sangha. We might want to establish a connection with certain people who have practised longer than us, and who can therefore mentor us. They will know us well enough to tailor their guidance to our individual needs and capabilities. Most of us will probably benefit greatly from such individual tuition, especially at certain junctures of our spiritual life. But we will also realize that we have much to offer each other; we all have valuable life experience and perspectives that are worth sharing. We can all have a positive influence on each other, helping each other better appreciate the creative possibility that dwells in all our lives.

myth and ritual
living in the diamond country

We cannot know his legendary head
with eyes like ripening fruit. And yet his torso
is still suffused with brilliance from inside,
like a lamp, in which his gaze, now turned to low,

gleams in all its power. Otherwise
the curved breast could not dazzle you so, nor could
a smile run through the placid hips and thighs
to that dark center where procreation flared.

Otherwise this stone would seem defaced
beneath the translucent cascade of the shoulders
and would not glisten like a wild beast's fur:

would not, from all the borders of itself,
burst like a star: for here there is no place
that does not see you. You must change your life.[23]

In the city where I live, the art gallery has a rather majestic Buddha statue. It is a standing Buddha figure from India, made of copper alloy, and larger than life size. The right hand of the Buddha is raised, with its palm facing outwards, towards us. This hand gesture (or *mudra*) is the gesture of fearlessness. For many years the statue was tucked away in a corner just outside the men's toilets. More recently it was moved to a much more prominent and appropriate position. In this new location, the visitor can catch sight of the Buddha from quite a distance, through several of the large halls. He is an impressive sight, conveying calm strength and confidence.[24]

Some time after the Buddha statue was moved, the gallery staff came to the Buddhist centre to ask for some of our brochures. They had received many requests from visitors for information about Buddhism. We also had a letter from a woman who'd called at the art gallery one day in her lunch hour. She was going through a difficult and painful time, and she went in just to get away from it all for a while. She wandered around and came to the room where the Buddha stood. The Buddha made a deep impression on her; a feeling of peace came over her, such as she'd not felt for a long time.

Such is the power of images. They can even move us to change our lives. Over the centuries, the Buddhist tradition has, like other world faiths, produced a wealth of spiritual art: images, texts, chants, statues, and architecture. Different branches of the tradition often have their particular style or form, but they are all created in order to try to communicate, or evoke, the qualities of Enlightenment. They are attempts to convey the peacefulness, confidence, compassion, or fearlessness that are potential in us all.

As we start to make our way along the Buddhist path and become interested in the Buddhist tradition, we might become more aware of these images and other works of art. We might encounter statues of the Buddha sitting cross-legged in meditation, or pictures of other Buddha-like figures of different colours, wearing jewels and silks, and holding various implements. In the Buddhist tradition there are stories dating back to the time of the Buddha, as well as writings of other Enlightened teachers, such as the poems of Kukai, the songs of Milarepa, or the devotional verses of Shantideva. There are the delicate and refined Chinese calligraphy and landscape painting, richly ornate Tibetan stupas, and the minimalist Japanese gardens. Some of these might appeal to us straight away, and some may seem rather strange, foreign, even unattractive. This wealth of material originates within cultures very different to ours: far distant in time and place. It is perhaps a question of learning the language they speak.

This chapter is about that language: that of imagery, myth, and symbol. How can we relate to the traditional Buddha images which we encounter in our explorations of Buddhism? What, if anything, have they got to do with our own way of life, our own sacred questions, living as we do in such a different time and culture?

You may also become aware of Buddhists bowing to statues of the Buddha, making offerings of flowers and incense, even praying to the Buddha. You might wonder what is going on here. Perhaps you were attracted to Buddhism because it is a non-theistic religion, and expected it to be free from superstition and ritual. Later in the chapter we will consider what ritual and devotion mean to a Buddhist practitioner.

the language of myth
Have you ever had the experience of wandering around an art gallery and finding that a particular painting jumps out at you? Perhaps you find yourself gazing at it for longer than others, and you go back later for another look. Or perhaps it's a certain poem that speaks to you more directly than any of the others in a book. You might not even know why. It might not become apparent until later – even years later. But there is a stirring in you: associations, thoughts, or feelings begin to awaken. There is a resonance between you and the painting or poem.

The painting or poem is speaking to you in the language of myth, of dreams, of imagination. You could say there are two basic languages, two ways of articulating an understanding about the world. One is logos: the language of reason, concepts, facts, and literal truth. The other is mythos: the language of myth, symbol, poetic and non-literal truth.[25] Each language has its own truth to convey. Each has its own mediums and domain in which its language can be learned and understood. It is no use reading the instructions for the washing machine as if it were poetry; you have to approach it logically, factually, step by step. On the other hand, you cannot really understand a painting by accumulating facts about it; you have to stop and look.

Buddhism speaks both these languages. It frequently speaks the language of concepts and reason, and tries to articulate the meaning of the teachings and the right way to practise them. If we are trying to travel along the Buddhist path, we need logos to understand clearly what it is we are trying to do, and where it is we are going.

The Buddhist tradition also speaks the language of myth and imagination in art, literature, and ritual. Sometimes mythos has an ability to speak to us on yet another level: it stirs deeper waters within us, it rekindles emotions, memories, and aspirations. It speaks to the unconscious depths and those aspects of us that just aren't going to be moved by a purely rational explanation of a teaching.

We often need to see things 'embodied' if we are to understand fully and get a feel for them. We may need to hear how to develop loving-kindness in a factual sense. But the story (in Chapter 11 below) of how the Buddha met with kindness a mother overwhelmed by grief, or a Buddha-image that seems to radiate serenity and compassion, convey the value and importance of loving-kindness in another, more dynamic, way. We see what the ideas about loving-kindness really *mean*. We get more of a 'felt' sense of what loving-kindness would be like when developed to its fullest pitch. The story or image is beautiful and therefore enjoyable, pleasing, and elevating. Words, forms, and colours are used to point us towards something beyond them.

I have sometimes taken part in workshops to help people enter the more symbolic language of Buddhist images. In one workshop we explored *mudras*: hand gestures depicted by certain Buddha figures. Each of these communicates a particular quality, such as fearlessness, meditation, generosity, or equanimity.

During this workshop people sat in pairs opposite each other, each adopting the gesture of a *mudra*. They didn't have any prior knowledge about what the individual *mudras* were or what they meant, but they were asked to notice the effect of performing a *mudra*, and of witnessing their partner's *mudra*. There was a noticeably different ambience in the room for each of the *mudras*. While everyone sat with their palms resting in their laps (the meditation gesture), the room became still and quiet. When people held their right hand up with palm facing outwards (the fearlessness gesture), there did seem to be an atmosphere of strength and confidence. By doing the gestures and getting a feel for them, the participants were able to guess what it was that each was trying to convey. This isn't magic, it's just language (although maybe you could say that language is magical). We communicate through gesture all the time. This workshop simply helped people to get in touch with that specific language of gesture.

So when approaching more traditional Buddhist imagery, it's a question of connecting with that mode or language. For example, we may come across a picture of a Buddha who is a deep ruby red, and looks at us with a kindly expression. He sits cross-legged on a huge lotus flower, and his hands rest gently in his lap, palms facing upwards. We might wonder who this figure is and why he is depicted in this way.

One approach to understanding the image is to read up on the traditional meanings, iconography, and symbolism. We discover that this Buddha is called Amitabha. His name means 'infinite light', and he is a Buddha who especially embodies love and compassion.

This helps us start to make sense of the meaning of the image, but we can also explore it in another way. We allow our own personal responses, associations, and connections to come to the fore. Do we find the picture attractive, or unattractive? Does it remind us of anything? What do we think it is trying to communicate, or embody?

So in the case of the picture of the red Buddha, we ask ourselves what associations we have with the colour red. A whole range of things might come to mind: love, fire, blood, wine, rubies, danger, warmth, heat, vibrancy, passion. We gaze at his expression and imagine what it might be like to meet such a person? And what about the way he is sitting – what does that communicate about him? We can feel free to have our own response to the image.

Then, when we know something about the more traditional symbolism, and we have considered our own responses and associations, the two can come together in a creative interplay. Contemplating this

Buddha helps us connect with the kindness that we wish to develop in our own lives. Basking in the warm, glowing red of Amitabha we intuitively feel what perfect compassion might be like. Noticing how he sits so still and grounded, legs perfectly folded, his hands resting in his lap, we also catch a glimpse of a calm strength. Somehow he has answers to our questions about life.

In the Buddhist tradition there are many such archetypal Buddha figures, in addition to the historical Buddha who lived 2,500 years ago, and they embody other qualities of Enlightenment, such as wisdom, energy, or fearlessness. Some Buddhists take up meditations in which they visualize these Buddha figures appearing out of the vast blue sky. There is not space here to go into the richness and magic of this way of meditating, except to say that, through these practices, they are trying to fire their imaginations and develop for themselves the spiritual qualities of these Buddha figures. They are entering the world of myth and archetype.[26]

exercise – *looking at the buddha*

Take some time to look at a picture or statue of the Buddha. Find an image in a book, or perhaps there is one at a Buddhist centre you attend or have access to. If there is a Buddha figure on the shrine at the centre or temple, you could go in early, sit quietly, and just contemplate it.

Try to dwell totally on the image, allowing time for it to sink in. Look closely at the body and its posture, and the face and its expression. If your mind drifts off, just bring it back, as you would in a meditation exercise.

Something to consider as you contemplate the figure is what it would be like to meet such a person. What is it that the image or statue conveys to you? Just allow an authentic response; don't feel you've got to like it!

Some people are more familiar than others with this world of myth and imagery. Allow yourself the freedom to explore wherever your interest takes you. If you are not at home with myth and imagination, do not worry about it. It might just take more time for the images to speak to you, or you may be drawn along the path by some other means.

Of course, it is not only Buddhist images that can communicate meaning and value. We might already have a relationship with images and myths of other cultures and traditions, including Western culture – which itself is a rich and vibrant tradition. We shouldn't feel that we must abandon our own culture once we begin to practise Buddhism. Actually, you can no more leave behind your culture than you can your genes. Many people, in fact, find that their love of their own culture grows deeper once they are following the spiritual path. They discover much that is of value. For example, like many people, I love the quality of compassion in the novels of George Eliot. She writes with such understanding of all her characters – the villains as much as the heroes and heroines. We are shown the circumstances and pressures that led to them to where they are now. Silas Marner, for instance, is a lonely, miserly, crabby, oddball of a man, but we can empathize with him, because of the way George Eliot tells his story.

As Buddhism takes root in the West, new images will gradually emerge. These will be a product of the interaction between three influences: traditional Buddhist imagery, the forms and myths of Western and other non-Buddhist cultures, and – most crucially – the spiritual experience of Buddhist practitioners. New insights and understandings will arise and convey themselves in different ways. Wisdom and compassion will find new mediums of expression, new forms in which they can be conveyed.

ritual and devotion

Another question might follow from all this. It is one thing to have images that communicate Enlightenment, but why do some Buddhists worship these images? We might be surprised to see Buddhists bowing to Buddha statues, offering incense to shrines, and chanting verses of devotion.

It is of course not the image, but the Buddha and his Enlightenment that Buddhists are revering. But why worship the Buddha? He wasn't a god, for there is no god in Buddhism. So why devotion and ritual?

Maybe we can explore this question with the help of an imaginary scenario. Perhaps you love reading and writing poetry. You have a favourite poet whose poems articulate to you most clearly and beautifully what you believe life is truly about. Her poems have made you think, they've made you laugh, and they've made you cry. You discover this poet is coming to your city. She will be reading poems and conducting a poetry workshop. You manage to get tickets for both events; you can't believe your luck.

The poetry reading is wonderful. The theatre is packed out with an appreciative audience. At the end there is warm and rapturous applause, and she is clearly much loved and an inspiration to many. At the workshop the next day you turn up along with about twenty other people. You were all at the reading last night, and you are all still inspired and uplifted. You're also a bit nervous about meeting your poet-hero face to face. You've been asked to bring along samples of your own poetry, but these feel rather inadequate now. You'll never be able to write poetry like hers!

When she arrives, a number of people express appreciation and respect for her work. She is grateful for this, but also down-to-earth. She asks you to get out your own poems and start working on them. Suddenly your feeling of nervous awe turns into excitement: you are looking forward to this opportunity to benefit from someone from whom you can learn so much. By the end of the day you feel even more uplifted, and more inspired to write your own poetry, in your own voice.

For Buddhists, the Buddha is a bit like the poet. He has eloquently articulated and clarified the meaning and potential of life. People naturally feel gratitude and a deep respect towards him, even a sense of awe, and they want to express it. However, like the budding poets at the workshop, they want to develop the wisdom and compassion of the Buddha for themselves; they want to move towards that ideal in their own lives too. They are keen to learn from the teaching and example of the Buddha and other Enlightened figures. They are expressing reverence for qualities that are also there, in them, at least in potential.

A Buddhist ritual, with the recital of verses, chanting of mantras, and offerings to a shrine, is a way of giving voice to this gratitude and reverence. We express our love and appreciation of these ideals because we are so glad they exist and are a possibility in the world. In this way, we are also affirming our desire, even our longing, to make them real in our own lives. This can be uplifting, and helps connect our emotions to our ideals. Rather than just being good ideas, our ideals become more deeply felt aspirations.[27]

Some people have a very positive experience of Buddhist ritual from their first introduction. But if we have had a difficult relationship with religion in the past, the idea of worship might be problematic for us. We may have had a previous experience of being asked to worship something we didn't believe in, or of feeling that religion promoted fear or guilt.

Or we might have an anxiety that ritual is cult-like, involving giving up our individuality and allowing ourselves to be taken over by the atmosphere and emotion of the group. There is no reason for it to be like this. Instead, it should be more like going to a concert where the music uplifts and inspires us. In a way, the music *has* swept us away and affected us deeply, but this has only happened because we have engaged our imagination. We are left feeling inspired, but also self-contained, more aware of our inner thoughts and emotions.

Devotion is an expression of our relationship with the Buddha. A relationship is a personal, organically evolving thing. We might hit it off with someone straight away, or we might take a long time to get to know them. Even if it takes a long time, the relationship can be deep and lasting in the end. It is not something we can do because we're 'supposed' to do it. For some, ritual is very important, for others it seems less necessary.

When we come to Buddhist ritual, we don't need to feel that we have to do it. If it doesn't mean anything to you, don't do it. We can join in, to an extent that is comfortable and appropriate for us. At some time we might want to see how we feel when we bow to the shrine, or offer some incense. It is worth experimenting.

I remember when I attended my first Buddhist ritual I was rather nervous about what it was going to be like. I made sure I was near the door in case I needed to get out quickly. The nervousness and uncertainty continued throughout, but at the same time I was deeply stirred by the words and the atmosphere. It certainly touched something in me that had not been touched before.

We may find we love ritual and enjoy its colour and beauty. Ritual involves enacting something with body (the posture we adopt, or bowing), speech (words and mantras that we recite or chant), and mind (our inner awareness of the ritual and its meaning). Because it includes all aspects of us in this way, it can be all the more powerful and meaningful.

In Chapter 1, we looked at the four reminders, a set of reflections designed to help us keep in mind what is really important and valuable about life. In a way, ritual has the same role. Through, for example, decorating and making beautiful the meditation space at a centre or temple, we are marking its importance and value, so that it stays special in our own hearts.

Here is an exercise about creating a ritual space in the room where you meditate at home.

exercise – *creating a ritual space*
You might like to build your own shrine at home – a special place where you can meditate. In a corner of a room, or on a shelf, you can arrange images and objects, Buddhist or non-Buddhist, that have significance to you. Or, before meditating, you might decide to chant, or read some verses, or poems that inspire you.

Try this and see what happens. Do you find that when you sit be-fore the shrine to meditate, you are reminded of your ideals and aspirations? Does having a ritual space help create an atmos-phere conducive to meditation?

the diamond country

We have been talking about the language of myth, and the images and words in which that language is spoken, but we can also see the whole world and all our environment as mythos. I once knew someone who would go camping on Dartmoor, which is probably the closest you can get to true wilderness in England. He would pitch his tent high on the moorland, miles away from anyone. He would feel the presence of the land and life around him. Sometimes he would feel this affinity to such a pitch that, if walking along a path he accidentally kicked a stone, he would stop, pick it up, and put it back in its place. This may sound like the act of a crazy man, but I find it incredibly moving. In a throwaway, consumer society, things only have value if we have a use for them. That use is often limited and short-lived, and after that they are of no value or interest. However, in some societies, everything is sacred, every object (even a stone) is full of significance and truth.

We probably couldn't live from day-to-day in the same way as my friend up on Dartmoor, but perhaps we can shift the balance a little way in that direction, away from a wholly utilitarian approach to life, towards an attitude of love and reverence towards all that lives. I think that is what a lot of us want and aspire to. We tend nature in our gardens, escape from the city into the countryside and up into the mountains. We travel to remote and fascinating corners of the globe. We contemplate paintings in art galleries, or lose ourselves in novels, films, and theatre. We want to dwell in the realm of myth. We want to be in places where our imagination roams free.

I once spent a month on a retreat in north-west Scotland. I stayed in a wooden chalet on a tiny beach. The hut was about ten yards from the water, and out in the sea were numerous small islands. During the whole month of my stay I did see a few people go by in boats, but only one man ever came down to the beach. It was midsummer and the days were long. The sun would hardly set; it just tilted under the horizon and rose again a few hours later. Sometimes I would wake at about 2am as the sun rose. The whole sky would be incandescent, velvet blue, and full of pale gold light.

I watched seals in the sea, and once saw a deer looking down at me from further up the cliff. I loved watching the sea birds. Fulmars would circle effortlessly round and round for hours. They would arc around and then up towards the cliff. You would think they were going to land – but no – at the last second they would change their minds and curve round again. It was as though they just loved that sweeping round and round. I would gaze into crystal-clear rock pools and watch hermit crabs feeding. I'd watch them transporting food to their mouths by passing it along a line of progressively smaller arms, to one tiny arm by their mouth that just flicked the food in. I'd converse with the gulls. Big, black-backed gulls would hang in the air looking down at me, saying, 'Wuck, wuck, wuck.'

It was not all idyllic. There were thousands of midges and the chemical toilet was not much fun to empty. But that month was one of the happiest in my life – although it was also one of the simplest. I felt in touch with a love and awareness of life. When our hearts are more full of love, we live in a beautiful world, a world of colour and magic. In such a world we are more in touch with a sense of awe and wonder, and everything seems alive, suffused with significance. Mindfulness – just watching – and loving-kindness are the keys to this world. Nature and beauty, myth and ritual, are doors through which we can enter.

This mythic world – the diamond country – is always there, always available to us. We can always travel to the diamond country, enter, and speak its secret language.

9

wisdom: one
the reflective life

In the office one day, someone says something that I find really irritating. Later that evening I'm playing and replaying our conversation in my head. I tell the story to myself about twenty times, each time embellishing it with more commentary and analysis of how utterly unreasonable they were. I think of all the clever, scathing things I wish I'd said. I fantasize about the final, irrefutable put-down I'll deliver when we meet tomorrow.

But another part of me wants to be able to put it to one side, to let it go. I become aware that I'm only perpetuating the irritation. I'm just causing myself more suffering. Why can't I just stop these thoughts going through my mind? It seems so perverse.

One answer is that, on some level, we believe that thinking this way, putting that person down, and establishing ourselves in a superior position, *will* make us happy. Deep down, we are not really convinced that letting go is the best thing to do, so we just can't do it.

This is what Buddhism describes as spiritual unawareness, delusion, even ignorance. All the many guises of negative emotion are misguided strategies for trying to make ourselves secure and keep suffering at bay. They are based on mistaken ideas about where happiness is to be found. These ideas, or views, are deep and subtle; we may not even know we hold them.

There is obviously nothing wrong with not wanting to suffer. The trouble is that we go about it the wrong way, and we actually end up by creating more suffering for ourselves. A vicious circle sets in, whereby delusion gives rise to negative emotion which then creates more delusion. For example, once we are in an irritable mood, it is likely that we will experience more people rubbing us up the wrong way. Our irritation causes us to exaggerate aspects of them we do not like and to discount their positive qualities. We simply do not see what is really there! What we observe around us becomes strongly conditioned by what is going on within us. Our perceptions are coloured by the mindset in which they occur.

By contrast, a state of mind in which our perceptions are not distorted, and in which we look with openness, clarity, and kindness, could be spoken of as wisdom. A wise person is one who, through this attitude of openness, can come to a better understanding of every situation he or she encounters. Such a person knows how to act appropriately, because they are able to find out more clearly what is *really* going on. They do not misconstrue a situation because of their own emotional biases. They are able to 'dwell in possibility', and to consider an issue from a number of points of view before making up their mind about it.

One of the key aims of Buddhist practice is to break that cycle of delusion and negative emotion, and to cultivate wisdom. This is what happened – to a far more radical degree – when the Buddha gained Enlightenment. He saw through delusion to a new, deeper understanding of life. He realized just how pervasively negative emotions poisoned our view of the world. Through meditation, gradually and systematically exploring his experience, free of spiritual ignorance, craving, and ill will, he was able to see things as they really are.

In the next chapter we will ask *what* we might see if we were to 'see things as they really are'. We'll explore how the Buddha could look at the world from another dimension, a totally different perspective. But in this chapter we will be considering *how* we might go about developing this greater understanding by looking at some practical tools for cultivating wisdom. The traditional framework we'll use to do this is known as the three levels of wisdom: listening, reflecting, and meditating. Then we will look particularly at methods of reflection and explore how the spiritual life is a reflective life. But first, a little more on wisdom and how it arises out of ethics and meditation.

the threefold path

The journey to Enlightenment is traditionally described in terms of a path of ethics, meditation, and wisdom. This threefold path gives a very simple overview of a whole lifetime of spiritual practice. First, we try to act ethically as we go about our lives. Ethical actions arise out of, and reinforce, positive states of mind – states of mind that are caring, generous, sensitive, and aware. So, when we come to the second stage, that of meditation, we have laid a solid foundation; we are already in a positive frame of mind, established in something like a meditative state. This allows us to take the process of transforming the mind a stage further by working on the mind directly – transforming the mind with the mind. We cultivate and nurture ever more aware and expansive states of consciousness.

Then, with a clear mind, free of emotional bias, we can see things more truthfully. Meditation becomes the foundation upon which wisdom can arise. In such a way, we move on to the third stage of the path and gradually train ourselves in wisdom.

But then the path circles back on itself. Our new understanding has implications for how we act in the world. We now see the world differently, so we want to respond to it differently. Wisdom leads back to ethics. In this way, the whole spiritual life can be seen as the ever-deepening practice of ethics, meditation, and wisdom.

Wisdom entails more than merely having the right concepts and ideas. It means understanding intuitively and deeply, with our hearts as well as our heads. In Chapter 1 we looked at the four reminders, the second of these being the reminder of impermanence. We all know that things don't last, but this doesn't prevent us being surprised, disappointed, or even angry when technical problems mean our train is cancelled, the sky suddenly clouds over, or a friend is unexpectedly taken ill. Although the idea of impermanence makes sense to us rationally, on a deeper level we do not understand it, nor even want it to be true. We *know*, but we don't *understand*. True wisdom is to understand on all levels of our being, rational and emotional. This was the wisdom the Buddha cultivated: he realized that he'd seen into life truthfully, fully, and completely. What he saw made such a profound impression on him that he knew this new understanding would prevail and always remain with him.

three levels of wisdom

The three levels of wisdom are essentially three different levels on which we absorb and assimilate a truth or insight that we have encountered or discovered.

The first level, listening, means encountering an idea through a talk or discussion, or by reading about it in a book. We come across a new insight in the form of words and concepts, ideas and information; we are interested in what it means and its significance in the story of our lives. When listening, we should feel free to ask questions, or read round a topic in order to clarify what we've heard. We want to ensure we've correctly grasped the idea that has been presented.

At the second level, that of reflecting, we absorb this truth more deeply. We take the idea more to heart, and make our own connections with it by mulling it over and looking at it from different angles. Does this idea make sense to us? Does it seem true? What are the practical implications for our own lives? Do we have a particular emotional response – be it one of inspiration or resistance?

We might reflect as we are reading, sitting quietly with a cup of tea, writing in a journal, or going for a walk. Many people find the gentle pace and rhythm of walking conducive to reflection.

When we're reflecting on a topic, the process of thinking it through can often continue in the back of our minds without our consciously willing it. Like a bubbling stew, we might just come over and give it a bit of a stir from time to time to check that it is cooking nicely and the flavours are improving. At other times we might reflect in a more structured way, pursuing a line of thought critically and rigorously. We can even reflect collectively. A study group can be useful in this way. Stimulated by discussion, a group of people may unearth insights that wouldn't have occurred to them individually.

Most of us could benefit from more reflection in our lives. It has been said that we tend to do an hour's reflection for every six hours of reading, but that it might be more fruitful to do six hours reflection for every hour that we read a book. We forget so much of what we read; we don't really take it in. But the more we reflect, the less superficial our reading becomes.

The third level of wisdom, meditating, takes this process of assimilation deeper still. We dwell on what we have learned in a less discursive, more intuitive way. We try to turn the *idea* into an *understanding*. We try to make it part of who we are and how we perceive the world. We allow the idea to sink into our hearts and minds, so that it has a transforming effect on us. We try to allow the idea to manifest in us and to be expressed through our lives.

Take the first of the four reminders that we explored in Chapter 1, that of the preciousness of human life. At first, we read about this in a book (listening). What we read suggests we consider the value and significance of our lives, and we go away and think about this (reflecting). We probably do think life is important and precious to us, but perhaps there are aspects of the reminder that cause us to reflect more. Do we make the most of the opportunities in our lives, or are there ways in which we waste them? Then we might take it further still by sitting quietly (meditating) and dropping some of these thoughts into our hearts. 'May I make the most of my life,' we say to ourselves. We try to let the idea sink down and touch us more profoundly, so that it has an effect on the person we are and the way we live our lives.

Or to take another example, we attend a Buddhist class and hear something about the loving-kindness meditation that makes us stop and think (listening). We realize we have built up unhelpful attitudes about certain people. Walking home after the class we dwell on these attitudes and resolve to change them (reflecting). In our meditation over the next few weeks, we bring these people to mind and try to cultivate loving-kindness towards them (meditating).

Each level of wisdom is progressively less discursive and more intuitive. As we move through the three levels – listening, reflecting, and meditating – we gradually make the understanding more deeply part of ourselves. But we shouldn't view the process too linearly. For example, we might have a profound insight in the midst of a conversation. Perhaps we are in a discussion group during a Buddhist retreat and somebody says something that strikes us very forcefully. It hits home, makes us sit bolt upright, and urges us to think. Maybe they've said something that is very pertinent to us, or it resonates with us, or inspires us. We might not even know why it seems so significant; that understanding might come later. I remember being on a study retreat, looking at a specific text about the Buddhist view of existence. We grappled with this text for several hours each day. After a few days I was having some of the most intense, 'filmic' dreams of my life. Although the study was predominantly conceptual and discursive, it still stirred up the unconscious depths of my mind. You never quite know when an insight might arise – an understanding full of significance for you might occur when you least expect it. The practice of wisdom therefore involves being as thoughtful and aware as we can – alive to the possibilities that are ever present.

really seeing

However, for the meditating level of wisdom, quiet and non-distraction become more essential. It is likely that this wisdom will only be developed while sitting in formal meditation. It will arise in its fullness only on the basis of very pure and concentrated meditative states, when distractions do not arise and the mind can be strongly focused.

There is a useful traditional distinction made between what are called *samatha* and *vipassana* types of meditation. *Samatha* means 'calm', and these types of meditation are those in which we purify and clarify the mind. The mindfulness of breathing and loving-kindness meditations are examples of these. *Vipassana* means '*really* seeing'. Vipassana meditations are about closely examining our experience on the basis of having developed calm and clarity, and therefore being more able to see what is really there. Samatha is like cleaning a lens of the grime that has accumulated on its surface. Vipassana is then being able to see through the lens clearly.

The Buddhist tradition has evolved many vipassana meditation practices that are specifically designed to cultivate wisdom in this way. For example, there is a practice in which one meditates on the six elements of earth, water, fire, air, space, and consciousness. One contemplates the presence of each element within oneself, and also how it came to be there and where it is next going. There is earth in me in the form of bones, skin, hair, teeth, and so on. But all this came from the world around me – from the food I have eaten, which came from the earth. The earth element also leaves me when I defecate, or shed old skin cells, or when my hair is cut. I strongly identify with my body and think of it as being durable and definitely mine. But the earth element does not belong to me. At death I will have to let go of it completely. By meditating in this way, we are able to pay close attention to our inner response to the ideas of impermanence and interconnectedness that we are contemplating. We may notice doubt or fear arising, but we are able to work to transform them. Or we feel a sense of liberation and release from identifying ourselves in a limited way. We can also feel more connected to the world – the sense of division between the world and us seems less rigid.

Observing the breath could also become a vipassana meditation practice. As we become closely attuned to our breathing, we notice that no two breaths are the same. In fact, we become aware how the idea of a breath is just an idea – what we really experience is a constant flow, an ever-changing process of coming and going, arising and falling away. Watching the breathing in this way might give rise to insights similar to those in the six-element meditation just described. We experience a feeling of giving and taking, and how we are connected to the air around us and other living beings. In some traditions it is said that when the Buddha gained Enlightenment, he was doing the mindfulness of breathing meditation.

ways of reflecting

In the remainder of this chapter we will examine the second level of wisdom in more detail. I'm going to suggest four different methods of reflection.[28]

circling around

First, we can just circle around a question or an idea. We allow associations, memories, stories, music, anything connected to the question to arise in our minds. We don't rule out anything that seems unexpected or even a bit off-beam. The process can have energy and a sense of fun. We could also put our thoughts on paper in the form of a mind map, or write down any teachings or ideas that seem relevant to the question. We don't edit ourselves, but allow the mind to roam around, making connections and uncovering new thoughts and feelings.

A writer on art has described how the process of looking at painting involves both reverie and contemplation.[29] Reverie is being attentive to one's own response to the painting. It means allowing ourselves to wander off into personal associations and memories. It may take time. We look at a painting and it appeals to us, but we can't quite say why. Something niggles at us as we gaze at that image. But if we allow time for reverie, an answer may emerge. Contemplation, on the other hand, means being attentive to what the artist painted. We look at exactly what is there on the canvas, and ask ourselves why it was placed there. We are trying to enter the world of the painting and its creator.

Reflection by circling around is a bit like that wandering reverie. For example, if we were reflecting on impermanence, we might note down how the idea of impermanence strikes us, recollect books we've read on the topic, remember how it was when a relative died when we were young, and so on. We range around the topic in the broadest way possible.

dropping a pebble into a still pool

Another way of reflecting is to sit in meditation and allow our minds to be like a clear, calm pool, and then to drop a pebble into that pool.

The pebble we drop in is a pithy idea, teaching, question, or even a quality that we wish to develop. It might just be one word, like 'impermanence'. We say the word quietly to ourselves as we sit in meditation and let it sink deep down into our hearts and minds. We watch the ripples caused by this pebble. How have we responded to what has been dropped in? Does it arouse feelings of fear or freedom? We can attend to these responses and then return to the phrase or idea we are contemplating if appropriate.

significant landscape

A third approach to reflection is to look at the world around us for clues, suggestions, or reminders connected to the issues and questions of our lives. We could be doing this kind of reflection all the time: on the bus, when eating, in the garden. For instance, we can always see examples of impermanence around us. To start with, this can seem a bit forced or clichéd, but eventually it becomes more natural and significant. Sometimes it is as if the landscape is speaking to us, has a message just for us. We gaze at the sea, for example, and it seems to speak to us of an indescribable openness and freedom. If we can practise awareness of our environment like this, we are able to take reflection into our lives, and this may help the ideas we are reflecting on really sink into us and not be forgotten. We are trying to see the truth of things reflected everywhere in all places and situations. (This is akin to the mythic approach described in Chapter 8.)

how to live, what to do

Finally, at some point in our reflections we need to come back to the practical implications for our way of life. What does this teaching, or that idea, demand that we *do*? How does it suggest that we should change our lives? If we have been reflecting on impermanence – to continue with that example – we might realize that there are practical implications. Our increased awareness of mortality and the fleeting nature of life make us realize that it would be good to make a will, to spend more time with an elderly relative, or to resolve a long-standing conflict with someone.

When reflecting in this way it is often good to be specific. It is too easy to come up with a well-meant but perhaps rather general, or unrealistic, resolution. Instead, we can carefully consider *what* it is we want to do, *when* we will do it, and with *whom*. For example, instead of a well-meaning exhortation to myself to be more aware of impermanence, it might be more beneficial to choose a small, but achievable instance of a circumstance in which I could do so. Once that is done, we can choose something else and develop the practice further.

exercise – *reflecting on your sacred question*

You could try some of these methods of reflection for yourself. Choose a question or topic that you would like to spend some time contemplating. It might be that you choose this by going back to the sacred question exercise in Chapter 1. Or you could take as a topic one of the four reminders from that chapter. Alternatively, there might be some other issue that is alive and relevant for you at present.

Then choose one of the four methods of reflection above and try it out over the next few days. Record what happens and anything you learn about the topic and also about the process of reflection itself.

If it seemed fruitful, you could then try considering the same issue using another method of reflection. Again, give this a few days sustained application. With reflection, it is good not to try to do too much too quickly, but to allow seemingly simple things adequate space and time.

the reflective life

So the cultivation of wisdom is a process of gradually assimilating an idea – asking if we find it to be true and useful in our lives, and, if we do, allowing it to have a transforming effect on us. It involves examining our experience in the light of that idea, and bringing the two – ideas and experience – into a creative dialogue.

This process doesn't always come naturally or easily. Our reflections can sometimes seem a bit artificial or abstract, or we can't really see the implications of an idea for our lives. Or when we meditate and nothing seems to happen, again it seems rather forced and unreal. But developing wisdom, like awareness, loving-kindness, or ethics, is a *practice*. It is something that comes to life gradually as we work at it.

Sometimes it is difficult *because* the practice is working! As we reflect, we might start to notice lots of distraction, resistance, or boredom, precisely because we are starting to get somewhere. The idea is beginning to sink in and our ego resists it. This is because we are attached to our views of the world. In a sense, we are made up of our views – they are the emotional and cognitive attitudes that allow us to navigate through the world. They give us our sense of who and where we are in the overall scheme of things. When such views are challenged we can find this very uncomfortable.

For example, perhaps we have been in conflict with someone and blamed him or her for something. Through reflecting on the matter, we are obliged to acknowledge that we played our part in the dynamic, but we resist this notion. Our self-view has been challenged, and this can leave us feeling rather rattled. The mind wriggles and tries to escape having to come to such an uncomfortable conclusion. It fills itself with distractions, and finds excuses and more reasons to blame the other person.

But we are only rattled while we remain identified with those views. If we are able to reassess and, if necessary, revise our view, then the discomfort disappears. We accept that maybe we could have responded to that person with more understanding, but we are able to forgive ourselves and move on. We realize we have some weak areas, but now we can learn to do better. So, if you reflect on something in particular and you notice a feeling of being stirred up in this way, it may actually be a sign of progress. You are starting to shake the foundations of your views.

If we have an emotional investment in a certain way of looking at the world, this view may be hard to unearth. We often don't see because we don't *want* to see. I may not notice someone's good qualities because it doesn't fit in with the view I have formed of them. As we saw earlier, the process becomes circular. We have an opinion of someone that means we see him or her in a certain way. Because we want to maintain this view, we have to filter out information that doesn't fit in, or interpret information in a way that reinforces our view.

In England, earthquakes are rare. I remember being on the seventeenth floor of a tower block when the building seemed to wobble. It happened in an instant. There was a jolt, and then everything was back to normal. My response to this was interesting. Buildings didn't, shouldn't, wobble. I couldn't believe it had happened. I didn't want it to have happened – it was rather disconcerting. So I started telling myself that maybe it hadn't happened. I must just have imagined it. Later I heard that there had been an earth tremor and I realized that this was what I had experienced. But, at the time, because it was not part of my view of things, I had tried to dismiss it.

Qualities such as openness, honesty, curiosity, and emotional positivity are required if we are to see things more truly as they are and develop wisdom. We need both an active and a receptive approach – deliberately working away at trying to understand, but doing so in a way that is open to new possibilities and ways of seeing. It may also require what Keats called 'negative capability' – the ability to dwell in a state of not-knowing, to be able to stay with 'uncertainties, mysteries, doubts, without any irritable reaching after fact and reason.'[30] Again, when we feel rattled we might hurriedly look for something to explain the problem away. We don't like to allow the problem just to be there, as not knowing is uncomfortable. However, if we think we know everything, there won't be any room in our minds for new understandings. When we are open to the idea of not knowing, new understandings can arise.

Wisdom will not come overnight; it is a lifetime's practice. We need to beware of assumptions and avoid coming to premature conclusions. We might take an idea such as impermanence and reflect on it for many years. It is important to take something that resonates with us, or that is a *problem* for us. It needs to be an idea, a teaching, or a symbol that relates to our sacred question. Over time, we will gradually unlock its hidden meaning and significance. Through gaining more experience and maturity in life, we continue to learn more about this burning question. We meet people who have their own insights to share. Books we read and films we see give us further understanding. It becomes a puzzle or dilemma that we are trying to solve: an underlying question that weaves its way through our entire lives.

exercise – *the reflective life*

How might you incorporate some ongoing element of reflection into your life and spiritual practice? Or is it already there and well developed? You could think about these questions in terms of the three levels of wisdom discussed above. Are there some levels that you do more to develop?

Consider bringing reflection into your daily meditation practice. This might be for a short part of your meditation each day, or only emphasizing reflection from time to time. Introducing a reflective element (such as the four reminders) can be especially useful if your meditation has become a bit dull and dry: the reflection can stimulate new ideas.

For some years, I reflected on impermanence because that was a problem for me. The sense that life was fleeting and therefore futile and meaningless was, in large part, responsible for bringing me to the spiritual life. But Buddhism told me that if I truly understood impermanence it could be liberating. I wanted to know what this meant. I wanted to find out if there was an answer, or whether it was all futile after all. I remember at times feeling baffled and bewildered, as if I'd never be able to understand, and, at the same time, a sense of exhilaration and wonder at the mystery of life. There were no easy answers, but a process of searching and enquiring that was immensely rich and satisfying. For me this is what life is truly about. And there are also, along the way, glimpses of further understanding. Reflection is not just hard work. It can also be exciting, inspiring, bringing with it a sense of freedom. There are occasional flashes of wisdom, intuitions of how it might be if we really understood the truth.

Socrates said that an unexamined life was not worth living. An examined, or reflective, life, on the other hand, is full of richness and wonder.

10

wisdom: two
the buddhist vision of existence

Hour after hour, day
After day we try
To grasp the Ungraspable, pinpoint
The Unpredictable. Flowers
Wither when touched, ice
Suddenly cracks beneath our feet. Vainly
We try to track birdflight through the sky trace
Dumb fish through deep water, try
To anticipate the earned smile the soft
Reward, even
Try to grasp our own lives. But Life
Slips through our fingers
Like snow. Life
Cannot belong to us. We
Belong to Life. Life
Is King.[31]

In earlier chapters, we heard how a young man on a spiritual quest – the man who was to become the Buddha – gradually developed his own way of meditating. He patiently trained himself, steadily transforming the complex of emotional attitudes and mistaken views of reality that he now believed were the cause of suffering. We are told that, on the full-moon night of May, after meditating through the night, as the morning star rose in the sky, the young man realized he'd seen through them all. He had at last found the Enlightenment that he had sought for so long. He had become a Buddha – which literally means 'one who is awake'. He had broken through into a new mode of consciousness and could now see things as they *really* were.

So how are things, really? How did the Buddha now see the world? After that profound meditation, when he finally opened his eyes, what was different?

exercise – *the nature of reality*

Without looking at the next few pages, write down how you would describe the 'nature of reality'. If you had to come up with a truth, or underlying principle, or even a law – like a law of science – that always holds true and describes everything, what would it be?

If your mind just goes blank, don't worry! After a while, you might be surprised what you come up with.

You can do this exercise even if you know the Buddhist 'answer'. Forget the Buddhism you know and come up with your own response. The point is not to get the right answer, but get us thinking about our underlying ideas and assumptions about the nature of existence.

Later, you can compare your principle with what the Buddha came up with. Are there similarities and overlaps? Or are there differences and contradictions?

It is also interesting to do this exercise with other people and compare your answers.

The principle used by the Buddha to describe reality was that of 'conditionality'. The Buddha said that every single event or object in the universe, when analysed, can be shown to be made up of causes and conditions. All phenomena are conditioned, and reality is this flow of causes and effects, which in turn become the cause for further effects. He saw this as quite natural – it was just the way things were.

When I first heard this law of conditionality it sounded rather dry, mundane, even disappointing. It wasn't what I was expecting would be the foundation of the spiritual vision of the Buddha (though quite what I was expecting, I'm not sure). My response was not like that of Sariputra, who was to become one of the chief disciples of the Buddha. When he first heard a similar explanation of conditionality, he had a spiritual realization on the spot.

No doubt this reflects my extreme spiritual denseness compared with Sariputra, but it is also a reflection that we live in a different time and culture. In the context of the Buddha's society, in which superstition still played a major part, the idea that all things proceeded according to natural laws must have sounded shocking and radical. But in our scientific age we have grown used to such a world-view and it can seem self-evident.

At least, we *think* it is obvious. But if we look more deeply at our assumptions about life, the Buddha's message remains just as radical. Unconsciously, we are still strongly inclined to see certain things as somehow separate from causes and conditions. Without even realizing it, we can harbour the hope or expectation that some things can be everlasting, completely satisfying, and inherently real.

However, the Buddha maintained the opposite, that all conditioned things are impermanent, ultimately unsatisfactory, and insubstantial. He suggested that many of our problems stem from our unawareness of these three facts of life. We try to live as though they were not true, or wish that we could somehow be exempt from them. This blindness sets in train a process of wrong thinking about the world that causes us to act inappropriately, and this, in turn, causes suffering, both for ourselves and for other people.

If, however, we *were* to understand the nature of things fully, free from all misapprehensions, we would have a very different experience. The Buddha also tried to describe what *that* would be like. For each of the three characteristics of existence, there was a corresponding description of how, if we saw deeply into that characteristic, we would experience reality. These are known traditionally as the three gateways to liberation. In this chapter we will explore each characteristic in turn, together with its corresponding gateway. We will see that, as we gradually awake to the true nature of things, we live more freely, dwelling in a greater possibility.

These gateways are important because they give us a sense of something positive to move towards. They affirm and make clear that the Buddha's message is one of spiritual freedom. On their own, the three characteristics might be interpreted as bleak and pessimistic, but they only describe reality from a certain viewpoint. If we look into them, and into reality, more deeply, we see things from another perspective.

When the Buddha *tried* to describe the enlightened experience of reality, he did so with some reluctance. It was very difficult. *Any* experience is difficult to express. Right now, I'm sitting in a room typing into a computer. If I tried to relate to you what the room is like, I could give you a rough idea. I could tell you about the colours of the walls, and the pattern of the fabric of the curtains, and you would start to conjure up an image in your mind's eye. But if you were later to see the room, it would probably not be as you had imagined. You might be able to recognize the room as that which I'd described, but it would still be quite different from how you'd pictured it according to my description.

Words and concepts are tools with which we try to convey an impression. They are tools a skilled writer or poet can use to communicate qualities and experiences in a wonderfully evocative way. But words can only evoke, hint at, or point us towards something; they cannot recreate that thing exactly.

If this is true when I describe my room, how much more so when the Buddha tries to describe his newly-discovered experience of Enlightenment. He knew that words could not adequately convey the subtlety and profundity of his insight. He was especially concerned that people might mistake a conceptual understanding for the real experience of Enlightenment.

Nevertheless, he did give some hints. We will look at these gateways to liberation, as well as at the three characteristics. But we would do well to remember that they are only hints, or suggestions, about the actual experience. We can only try to imagine and get some feeling for what the experience of awakening *might* be like. We should perhaps bear in mind that, like the room we imagined, the reality will be somewhat different.

impermanence

The first characteristic of existence is that of impermanence, which we have already come across in other parts of this book. The Buddha said that one implication of things being conditioned, of being contingent for their existence on other conditions, it that everything is constantly changing. Some things change from moment to moment, others change slowly, over millions of years. But they are all, always, changing.

I remember one experience of impermanence that made a particular impression on me. I was staying on my own in a little stone-built cabin at Guhyaloka, the retreat centre in Spain I described in an earlier chapter. It sits in a valley flanked by huge limestone cliffs. These rocks are millions of years old and have a feeling of timelessness about them. One night I was sitting meditating when I heard a loud noise: smashing, sliding, scraping. It sounded as if something big was sliding down the hill. My first thought was that a car had slid off the road and was crashing down the terraces into the valley. But the noise continued and I realized it was quite near and getting louder. I raced outside with my heart pounding. The noise stopped. I flashed my torch around in the dark, but I could neither hear nor see anything. All I could do was go back inside, my heart still thumping.

The next morning, I could see what had happened. A boulder about two metres wide had fallen from the cliff. Its trail of destruction as it had hurtled down the scree slope was clearly visible. Trunks and branches of holm oak trees were split and splayed out either side of its path. On the road below there wasn't a mark, so it must have bounced straight across. On the opposite side were more split branches, smashed walls, and huge gashes in the ground. About twenty yards from my cabin lay the boulder. Its path looked pretty much in line with the cabin.

The occupants of the retreat centre hadn't heard of such a thing happening before, and attributed it to exceptionally wet weather. But it gave me food for thought. Those impassive ancient cliffs were not so permanent after all, and I nearly wasn't as permanent as I'd assumed either.

On some level we can think that we, and other people and other things, are permanent. Or at least we wish it could be so. We want those people and experiences we like and enjoy to go on for ever. But it cannot be.

exercise – *seeing into impermanence*
Jotting down thoughts and impressions as you go, sit quietly and reflect on what our experience might be like if we fully understood that things are impermanent.

If you really knew that nothing lasts for ever, how would you relate to the world around you, and to other people? What would your moment-to-moment experience be like? How would you live your life?

As in the first exercise, you might be surprised by what you come up with if you give it time.

intimacy with all things
If we understood that everything is fleeting and constantly changing, we might develop a greater appreciation of the preciousness of things. We would have a much stronger sense of the value of the present moment. We would know that, in a sense, each moment is all there is: the present moment flowing into the next. Perhaps, with this awareness, we would be closer to things: seeing, tasting, and experiencing the flow and flux of life with more immediacy. We might live each experience more fully and vividly.

The Buddha described this gateway to freedom, which we enter when we see deeply into impermanence, as the 'imageless'. To unpack this, we need to go back to an earlier point concerning the limitations of words and concepts. Words, ideas, and labels are crucial for under-standing and communicating the world, but sometimes we see the label instead of the real thing. We see the signifier, instead of what is signified.

We may often do this with people. We get to know someone and we form an idea, or image, of them. There is nothing wrong with this as far as it goes. But sometimes we start seeing the image instead of the person. This person may change, but our image doesn't keep up with the change. We see them in the same old way – because we are not actually seeing them, but the label. Our idea of someone hardens into a set of assumptions and fixed ideas. Parents and children often do this in relation to each other. Children grow up fast and become young adults, but their parents' image of them cannot keep up with the change. In subtle ways they still view the young adult as a child. The young person also struggles to relate to their parents in a new way, and may slip into old ways of communicating, which then re-inforce the parents' outdated image of them.

If, however, we are really in touch with the changing nature of things, if we are consequently in a more vivid, moment-to-moment aware-ness of impermanence, then we see the thing itself, and not the label, name, or image. The expression 'thinking outside the box' means the ability to think in new ways, free of old assumptions. Experiencing imagelessness, we think, and also see, hear, taste, touch, and smell, outside our unconscious assumptions that a thing will be like *this*, be-cause that is what it has always been like. 'Outside the box' conveys this well – we create a box for ourselves. Instead of being suggestive or evocative, ideas and labels imprison us and we can't see outside them. Instead of words and concepts being tools by which we can gain a better understanding of the world, they blinker us.

In experiencing things as imageless, we taste them, from moment to moment, in all their inherent freshness, immediacy, uniqueness, and

137

purity. We have all had episodes in our lives that gave us a hint of what this might be like. Maybe you can recall some such times now. What kind of situations conduce to this sense of vividness?

I remember the first time I went to a foreign country, flying to Alicante in Spain and leaving behind a greyish April day in England. As I emerged from the plane, I was immediately struck by a whole range of sensations. The heat hit me the second I stepped from the plane. The sky was an intense blue. Even the smell of the hot tarmac in my nostrils was different to what I'd left behind.

As we left the airport, and I looked out the car window, everything was different. Even ordinary things like lampposts, road-signs, and telegraph poles weren't the same as in England. A flock of hoopoes flew by – another new experience. We drove though fields and orange groves and the sweet smell of orange blossom filled the air. I was happy and excited. Everything was so fresh and vivid. I was having an experience of what in Zen is called 'beginners mind' – experiencing things free of preconceptions and expectations.

But we do not usually sustain this heightened awareness for very long: things soon become familiar and greyed-over in our perception. But to have a full appreciation of impermanence would be to live in this heightened way all the time. Dogen, a Zen master of thirteenth-century Japan, was once asked what Enlightenment was like. His reply was that it was 'to be intimate with all things'.

We can also get a sense of what this state of imagelessness means by watching what happens when we do the mindfulness of breathing meditation. When we start watching the breath, it is often as though we are 'up here' in our head, looking 'down there' at this thing called the breath. We start looking down into our body for various sensations that we expect to be there because they were there the last time we watched our breath.

So what we can end up looking at is our idea of what the breath will be like, rather than the breath itself. Our experience of the breath is consequently a sort of construct. But this changes as we gradually become more mindful and absorbed. It becomes less like observing from outside. We are not really thinking about an idea of the breath any more, or about an idea of our watching the breath. There is just the pure, immediate, and ever-changing flow of the breath itself – experienced directly.

unsatisfactoriness

The second characteristic of existence is that things are unsatisfactory. Here the Buddha is bringing out further implications of conditionality and the first characteristic. Because we live in a world that is complex and ever-changing, things are never going to work out exactly how we want them. There are just too many variables at work, too many conditions at play, to expect them to turn out just right. We want it to be sunny, but it rains. Even if it is sunny, the local farmers will be disappointed, as they wanted it to rain. The nature of the world is that it can't give us what we want, at least not completely, not all of the time.

But on some unconscious level we don't want this to be true. Somewhere within we hold onto the hope that life *should* work out exactly the way we want. Watching our inner dialogue, we can often catch ourselves longing and expecting in this way. If only we had this, or if only that person would do that, *then* we would be happy. We can latch onto one thing that, in our imagination, becomes the sole condition for our future satisfaction.

The Buddha does not deny that there are pleasurable experiences, or say that there is no satisfaction at all to be gained from the world. But he observed that nothing ever satisfies us *completely*. On a physical level, things just go wrong: illness takes hold of us, disasters strike, or there is simply the physical discomfort of being too hot or too cold. On a psychological level, there is the stress and annoyance of trying to get the world put to rights, or the worry that something will come along to mess up what you've just managed to achieve. On a more existential level there can be an intuitive sense of the futility of this constant struggle. There is a feeling that even when we do get things the way we want them, they still don't fully satisfy our deepest longings. Something in us still feels empty and yearns for fulfilment. Our nature is that we, too, are ever changing, and this means that we are greater in potential than we imagine, so that even getting what we want will never completely satisfy us.

The Buddha isn't calling for a pessimistic attitude to life. Nor is he promoting a passive stoicism or saying we shouldn't improve those aspects of life we are able to control or influence. He is simply bringing to our attention the fact that we will never be able to control the world entirely to our satisfaction.

exercise – *seeing into unsatisfactoriness*

Jotting down thoughts and impressions as you go, sit quietly and reflect on what your experience might be like if you fully understood that things are unsatisfactory.

If you really knew and accepted that worldly things depend on conditions and are always changing, and therefore can't give us complete and lasting satisfaction, how would you relate to things around you, and to other people? What would your moment-to-moment experience be like? How would you live your life?

Again, you might be surprised what you come up with if you give it time.

unbiased equanimity

Perhaps, if we have a fuller understanding of this truth of unsatisfactoriness, we will approach life with different expectations. If we know that things don't always work out perfectly, we won't be surprised or shocked when they go wrong. Whatever path we take will involve some problems and difficulties along the way. There is no such thing as a perfect solution. This should not prevent us trying to find the best solution, but we know that, whatever course of action we take, it will have some consequences that we didn't intend or foresee. Knowing this helps us to be a bit more relaxed in our approach to life. We don't have to get everything 100% right.

There are some people, however, who go to the other extreme. To protect themselves from disappointment, they hold a dismissive attitude and pretend they don't really care. For example, someone applies for a job they would really love, but they are not confident, so they go about airily telling people that they aren't bothered if they don't get it. This results in their not making their best attempt to get the job. A better attitude would not be such a cool indifference, but an honest equanimity. They would try their best, but be prepared to accept the outcome, whether they got the job or not.

The Buddha called the gateway to the freedom experienced when we fully understand the truth of unsatisfactoriness, the 'unbiased'. It is a profound equanimity, a radical freedom from unrealistic expectations. Things will be as they will be. If we adopted this perspective, we would give ourselves to life, do what we could to be responsible and plan for the future, and then accept what happens. We would not get ourselves in a panic, worrying about situations that might never arise.

Even with this attitude, we cannot avoid all suffering. The Buddha still suffered physically from illness and old age. But he didn't suffer from the other layer that we often add to our suffering. When something goes wrong we can suffer more because we resent it and resist it; we tell ourselves that it isn't fair, or we want to know why it is always happening to us.

I remember once camping out in bad weather. It was cold and wet, and there was no way to escape the elements. I sat in my tent feeling miserable. At some point, however, I realized this was not helping. There was nothing I could do to change the weather; I just had to accept it. At that moment, something inside me just let go. I had been tensed up, resisting reality, and trying to keep it out. This only caused more discomfort – it made it feel worse than it actually was. Once I let go, my experience changed – the sensations of cold and damp were just sensations; they didn't seem nearly as unpleasant.

So in the freedom of the 'unbiased', we are open and accepting of whatever situations, emotions, and experiences arise, rather than shrinking back into a smaller, tighter version of ourselves.

insubstantiality

The third characteristic of existence also goes into the implications of conditionality, this time in a more philosophical manner. We tend to forget conditionality and think of things as being permanent and substantial, separate from everything else. But if things are made up of causes and conditions, they can have no fixed nature, no substantial core that exists separately from other phenomena.

The Buddha called this insight 'insubstantiality'. The things that seem so real and solid to us are actually a flow of ever-changing conditions. It's a bit like the images we see on our TV screens: in reality there is nothing there at all, just points of light flashing quickly on and off.

This might be philosophically interesting, but why does it matter? The Buddha addressed this issue because he could see that our idea of a separate and substantial existence of things *is* a problem. It creates difficulties and limitations in how we relate to the world.

The Buddha said it especially causes problems when we have an underlying assumption of the existence of a fixed, separate self, the idea of which he denied. He insisted that, just as much as anything else, everything associated with us is a process of change.

It might sound as though the Buddha is saying that we don't really exist. But, as with the other characteristics of existence, if we really see into insubstantiality we arrive at another perspective. We enter a doorway into a deeper freedom.

Other philosophers around at the time of the Buddha claimed they had found how to discover the true self. The Buddha went the other way and declared there wasn't one! But, strange as it might seem, he believed this was the way to emancipation. He saw that much of the suffering we undergo was owing to constantly having to maintain and defend this sense of self. If only we could let go of the notion of a self that is somehow apart from, or behind, the flow of conditions in the mind, we would experience enormous relief and liberation. Moreover, this fixed self-view limits us: we over-identify with a restricted idea of who we are, not realizing our true potential and the possibility of change.

In a sense, everything that happens to us – all the thoughts, worries, fantasies that flicker in and out of the mind – doesn't need to worry us. It is not really 'us'. None of it is completely, finally real; it is just a flow of conditions. Rather than identify with it as 'me', we can have a much bigger sense of 'ourselves'.

We do exist. We do have individual personalities, histories, and relationships. It is just that we don't need to over-identify with any of this, to completely pin it down and say things like, 'I'm only able to be *this* kind of person,' 'I only do *these* kinds of things,' or, 'I only get on with *those* kinds of people.' We would then have a less fixed, limited, and habitual view of ourselves.

Maybe we can see that we have fixed ideas about both ourselves and other people. It would be difficult not to have any ideas and opinions about people, but we need to recognize that they can change too. Our views can only be provisional working hypotheses, otherwise we box people in, limiting them and ourselves. For example, our self-view often lags behind who we really are. It needs to catch up with the person we have become. Sometimes we spot an out-dated view of ourselves. For example, I notice I'm dealing with a tricky situation and realize that two years ago this would have made me distinctly anxious. But now I don't feel any anxiety at all. I need to update my view of myself as an anxious person. It can be so encouraging to realize that we are not the person that we thought we were, and that we can change, and have done so.

We might also notice ways in which we can keep our view of others more open. I have a friend who began to sense that his view of his children was becoming rather fixed. He thought this was because he was getting older and tending to settle down in his views and assumptions, and also just getting used to the children always being there. But they were also getting older and moving into adolescence, becoming more self-conscious and aware of their appearance to others. This meant that there was a certain freshness and spontaneity of childhood they were growing out of, and this exacerbated his tendency to fix them in his mind. He realized he wanted to make sure he kept his attitude to them – and to who they were deep down – open-minded and not fixed.

exercise – *seeing into insubstantiality*

Jotting down thoughts and impressions as you go, sit quietly and reflect what your experience might be like if you fully understood that things are insubstantial.

If you really knew that nothing is fixed and separate, how would you relate to things around you, and to other people? What would your moment-to-moment experience be like? How would you live your life?

If this feels a little too abstract, think about your own self-view and your view of others. Are there specific examples, like those given above, in which you can see you've fixed your view of someone? Are these views always helpful? What would it be like to hold such views more fluidly?

openness and freedom

Perhaps, if we could see people and things as always being in a process of change, and therefore never fixed and finalized, we would sense their openness and ever-present potential for transformation.

This gateway to liberation is indeed called the 'openness' or the 'empty'. It is empty of any fixed, substantial nature. Any idea we have about the nature of something is only part of the story. Its true nature is actually much more vast and mysterious. When we have this wisdom we are open, in the sense of being alive to the ever-changing nature of reality. We are therefore receptive, flexible, and creative in our attitude to life. From this dimension, we see the world as open, dynamic, and full of possibility. The word 'Buddha', which literally means 'awake', suggests a keen alertness to the potential for transformation of all things.

In later Buddhist tradition, this openness came to be symbolized by the image of the blue sky: vast, expansive, unlimited, and pure. At the same time, it is full and shimmering. Out of this blue sky all things appear and then disappear. Reality is mysterious and unknowable. Who can say where things come from and where they go?

Last autumn I planted daffodils in my garden, and this spring they have grown out of the ground and burst into bright yellow flowers. From where did that yellow come? If I cut a bulb open, I would not find yellow, but a wizened brown skin and greenish white flesh inside. There is no yellow in the black earth, or in the rain that fell. You could say that the yellow comes from the genetic structure of the plant. In a sense it does, but the genetic structure is a long, complex chain of molecules – there is nothing yellow there either. Where did the yellow come from? And where does it go when the flowers wither, turn brown, and rot away?

The universe seems to be a mysterious process of things constantly appearing, disappearing, and reappearing. Although science can tell us a lot about how this works, it only goes so far. It can describe how, as the plant grows, the cell structure changes into one that reflects yellow light. But from where did that different cell structure come? Science is very effective at describing the process of cause and effect, but there is a level on which *how* one thing leads to another remains rather mysterious.

The point of all this is that if we are in touch with the openness of things, in touch with a sense of wonder and dwelling in possibility, then we can contact a much more creative, dynamic attitude to life. We know we can change. We know we – and others – are not fixed. We become free. It is the blue sky that makes Enlightenment possible. If it were not for conditionality and impermanence, no Buddhas could ever exist.

In other words, the three characteristics may seem from our viewpoint rather disappointing, disconcerting, even frightening. We wish that they might not be true. But from the vantage point of a Buddha, they are liberating truths – they allow for that dwelling in possibility that is Enlightenment.

How would one live, once one had developed such wisdom? How would such a person act in the world? In the following chapter, we will further explore the implications of the wisdom of the Buddhas. We will see how compassion also flows out of this truthful under-standing of life.

11

compassion
the kind heart of wisdom

Compassion is far more than emotion. It is something that springs
Up in the emptiness which is when you yourself are not there,
So that you do not know anything about it.
Nobody, in fact, knows anything about it
(If they knew it, it would not be Compassion);
But they can only smell
The scent of the unseen flower
That blooms in the Heart of the Void[32]

When Siddhartha left home in search of Enlightenment, he did not go because he wanted a trouble-free life. He wasn't looking for an easy way out, or avoiding responsibility. To leave behind everything safe, comfortable, and familiar and go off into the unknown and into the forests – dangerous places full of wild animals – must have taken a lot of courage. His sheer perseverance through all the years of struggle – including travelling up numerous blind alleys – showed that he must have had great determination and self-confidence, as well as an urgent need to find the answers he was looking for.

Why did he do it? Why did he have to leave everything he knew and go off like that? In the previous chapter, we looked at the three characteristics of existence that Siddhartha understood when he did finally attain Enlightenment. But, in some way, he had always known about impermanence, unsatisfactoriness, and insubstantiality. This was what had spurred him on in his quest. These 'facts of life' troubled him and kept him awake at night. They raised all sorts of questions that

147

worried him in the background of his mind, and would not go away until an answer had been found. He saw these three unavoidable truths all around him. However much he tried to distract himself, he couldn't forget them.

He was aware of so much suffering in the world. In India at that time, sickness would have been much more common than in wealthy countries today. He had never known his own mother; she died when he was just a few days old. Although in many ways he was happy, he could not deny the fact that everything that was dear and familiar to him was also fleeting and would one day be taken away. The finery and luxury his family could afford, the games of his youth, and the promises of a bright future – he could see through it all. He knew that even his family and friends would all have to part from each other one day.

As he grew older, he realized the lovely world of his childhood was a dream. The real world was much less innocent. From his father he heard of feuds between local tribes – bitterness and hatred, greed and corruption. He felt a deep sense of futility. He knew he couldn't spend his life in this way. He had to try to find something better – for himself, but also for his friends and those he loved. He couldn't just stay there, only to watch them all caught up in this endless struggle.

Although he had always had some understanding of the three characteristics of existence, it was not until he gained Enlightenment that he fully understood them. As we saw in the previous chapter, he then looked at them so deeply that he saw right through them, and into another, completely different, dimension. He was able to pass through the three gateways to liberation.

Thus, right from the start, the Buddha's quest was motivated by compassion. It was an acknowledgement of his own sense of futility and also a feeling for the suffering inherent in the world that inspired his search. And, as we saw in an earlier chapter, once he had found his answer the Buddha went back to the world. He acted out of compassion. He wanted to help others step through that doorway into freedom.

Enlightenment is described as the development of perfect wisdom and compassion. Wisdom is the inner understanding and vision of reality. Compassion is the activity that follows from that understanding. Wisdom sees that others suffer because they do not yet understand reality. Compassion is aware of that pain and suffering, and does what it can to help others escape it.

Later in this chapter we will ask how, in practice, we can begin to develop such compassion. Before that, we will explore a little more the relationship between compassion and the wisdom of the previous chapter. But first, we hear of an encounter between the Buddha and a grief-stricken mother.

the story of kisa-gotami

One of the best known stories about the Buddha is that of his encounter with a woman called Kisa-Gotami.[33] After many years of wanting a child, Kisa had recently given birth to a baby boy, but, tragically, he had died. She was utterly distraught, almost mad in her grief. She could not accept what had happened. Clutching the little child, she wandered round the village looking at people with her beseeching eyes and a panic-stricken face. Was there nothing they could do to help? Why would they not *do* something? But the villagers did not know what to do. Some tried to comfort her, but could not get close to her in her wretched state. Some were embarrassed by her show of emotion, and wanted to avoid her. Some felt for her, but were at a loss for words. Eventually someone suggested that she could go and talk to the Buddha, who happened to be staying near the village at that time.

Kisa's eyes lit up. Perhaps this 'Buddha' could do something to help. She hurried off, still carrying the dead child. Across the fields there was a well-known glade, and this was where the Buddha was staying. She could see who he must be – that man sitting in the middle of the circle of trees, surrounded by other monks and people from local villages. The Buddha saw her too. He looked carefully at her face, saw the dead child under her arm, and took it all in. He beckoned for her to come up to him, and people moved to one side for her to approach.

'Can you help me bring my child back?' enquired Kisa. 'Yes,' said the Buddha, 'I can help you, but on one condition.' 'What is that?' cried Kisa, eager to know, but worried there might be some catch. 'All I need is some mustard seed,' replied the Buddha. Kisa was overjoyed. Any household in the village would have mustard seed. The job was as good as done. 'But,' continued the Buddha, 'it must come from a house where no one has died.' 'Yes, yes,' cried Kisa, who was only half listening and already rushing off on her errand.

Back in the village Kisa went straight to the woman sitting in the doorway of the first house. She asked for mustard seed and the woman was happy to give her some. But then Kisa remembered she also needed to check that no one had died in that house. 'Ah,' said the woman, 'well that's different. My old father passed away in this house just last year.'

Kisa went to the next house where a man told her his daughter had died two years ago. She tried other houses, but everywhere it was the same. Everyone was happy for her to have some mustard seed, but every household had also known death at some time.

Halfway up the path to the next house Kisa slowed and came to a stop. She realized why the Buddha had sent her to get mustard seed. She understood that everyone knows death; it wasn't only her who had experienced such loss. She saw that, painful as it was, she had to accept what had happened and let her little child go. Suddenly the sadness welled up inside her and she burst into tears. Now she could let her grief flow forth.

A few days later, back in the glade, the Buddha saw Kisa approaching again. She looked different: her heart was still grieving, but there was also a calmness about her. She was no longer carrying her child. In the last few days she'd arranged the funeral and cremation, and now she wanted to come and follow the Buddha.

This story is a beautiful illustration of the Buddha's combination of wisdom and compassion. He had the wisdom to see what was troubling Kisa, and, furthermore, to find a means by which he could help her see what was going on. He had the compassion to act on this and not flinch from showing her a difficult and painful truth. The story teaches us that possessing compassion gives us the ability to see into the truth of pain and suffering, and stay there with that pain. We cannot bear too much reality, or we rail against it in anger, but the compassionate heart sees it all, and carries on loving.

wisdom and compassion

In other words, wisdom, a true understanding of how things are, leads naturally to a compassionate response to the world. Acting compassionately, out of concern for others, is to act in accordance with reality.

In the previous chapter we explored the idea of conditionality: that all things are made up of causes and conditions. This means that they are always subject to change and transformation. But sometimes we are in denial of this fact of existence. We try to pin down the conditions of our lives exactly how we want them, in the hope that this will give us total satisfaction. We also pin down our view of ourselves, holding tightly to fixed, limiting ideas of a self. The Buddha said that this, sooner or later, leads to disappointment and suffering. But if we live in wisdom, in harmony with life and the reality of things, then we live with an expanded, open, flexible sense of ourselves. Wisdom entails living in this way, and compassion involves doing what we can to help others to live in this way, so as to minimize suffering.

The Buddha helped Kisa see how she was fighting reality. Accepting the truth of her situation was painful, but much less so than to go on fighting. The Buddha is suggesting that we are suffering unnecessarily much of the time, not just at those more crucial life situations. We are asked to look at the thoughts that are going through our minds on a minute-by-minute basis. Are those little distractions, irritations, or fantasies also based on unrealistic views of the world?

exercise – *our sense of self*
Maybe we can actually feel this quite physically and tangibly in our own experience. If you are in a state of ill will, you can ex-

151

plore this in meditation. What is the experience actually like? How does your sense of 'self', or 'me', feel? Does it feel expanded or contracted, tight or relaxed, open or closed, pleasurable or painful? Where in the body do you feel this?

Likewise, when you are in a state of generosity, or friendliness, how does this feel? Does it feel expanded or contracted, tight or relaxed, open or closed, pleasurable or painful?

Buddhism is suggesting that to act unethically and without compassion is to be out of harmony with the way things really are, which is why acting like this is painful. This is when we are acting from a small, fixed, sense of self. Perhaps we can see from our own experience that this is what ill will feels like. We feel small, tight, or constricted in our heart or guts when we are angry, stubborn, or frustrated. Acting from such a small sense of self, we see only our own needs – in a narrow way at that – and not the needs of others.

But ethical actions and compassion are in tune with reality. When our idea of our self is more flexible and fluid, and therefore much bigger, the boundaries between self and other become more permeable. Loving-kindness is expansive in this way. It may be a physical experience. We might feel more open, warm, and relaxed. We are more able to consider the needs of others. We feel more able to give, rather than merely to take. We are freer and happier.

In the story of Buddhism, we have seen that compassion was the ideal right from the start. It was part of Siddhartha's motivation for setting off on a spiritual quest. Later, when he had gained Enlightenment, he taught others and a community of disciples accumulated around him. And once they were sufficiently experienced and confident, he exhorted them to travel off in different directions 'for the welfare of the many'.

Later in the Buddhist tradition, this compassionate ideal was expressed through the idea of the Bodhisattva. A Bodhisattva is one whose life is dedicated to relieving the suffering of other beings, and who realizes that Enlightenment – the consummation of wisdom and compassion – is what will best enable them to achieve this. They pursue the spiritual life deeply motivated by altruism and compassion.

developing compassion

I once accompanied a friend to hospital for some injections into his spine. Before starting the treatment, the doctor warned him that they would be extremely painful. My friend lay on the couch and I stood next to him. He was a fiercely independent man. He'd been a bit of an outsider most of his life, and in some ways he didn't like depending on other people. However, as the first injection went in, he cried with pain and his hand stretched out towards mine. This reaching out was quite a move for such a proud man to make. But, for some reason, I hesitated for a second. Maybe I was surprised, maybe I felt awkward. And, in that instant, he pulled his hand back. I always regretted that momentary hesitation.

Compassion is a beautiful ideal, but it is not always easy. Sometimes, we do not want to be aware of suffering, so we try to ignore its existence and look the other way. Or, in more subtle ways, we hesitate, or hold back, because we think that to be with someone in pain will itself be painful. Or maybe we do allow the awareness in, but we are overwhelmed by it, thinking we have to be able to make the suffering go away, or that there's just too much suffering in the world to cope with. So we can fall into an anxious, fretful state that is no use to anyone, or we can become burnt-out, or even – if the pattern carries on over time – weary and cynical.

How can we work against these tendencies? This is a big topic, and what follows are just some initial, brief, suggestions. First, we can distinguish between what are called our sphere of influence and our sphere of concern. The former is the sphere in which we can act and make a difference in the world. The latter is the sphere in which we are concerned about people, but also in which some things are beyond our control. If we are not aware of the distinction between these two, we can quickly become overwhelmed by the sheer scale of suffering in the world and our inability to do much about it. We then fall into the anxious or frustrated states in which we can't even do that which is within our sphere of influence. It is helpful to maintain an awareness of this distinction. Then we can try to expand our sphere of concern and keep it as open as possible. At the same time, we know that our sphere of influence is bound to be smaller, but we can still do those things that fall within it. This is what compassion is: a consciousness that is open and expansive and therefore aware of suffering. It comes into, and stays in, relationship to suffering, even when it cannot personally influence it, although it will do what it can.

Secondly, we recognize that to cultivate compassion requires loving-kindness towards oneself. It requires emotional robustness and strong inner resources of positivity to bear with suffering in this way. So the time we take to develop loving-kindness – including towards ourselves – is time well spent. We will need to invest in ourselves in this way if we are to act as a force for good in the world. We could even see the first stage of the loving-kindness practice as giving compassion and empathy to ourselves: we are listening to our inner thoughts and emotions with a kindness and concern. We listen and try to understand why we think and feel in this way. Listening carefully, we can sometimes experience a sense of release.

Thirdly, we can try to learn empathy. When confronted by someone's suffering, we can feel awkward, thinking we've got to make the suffering go away. Well, if there is something practical we can do, let us do it. But sometimes we can't remove the suffering. Sometimes we can't *do* anything, but we *can* just be there with the person, bearing witness with them. It is this 'being with' that allows someone to know that they are loved. They are not completely alone, but are connected to another person. Knowing this can make all the difference to them. Often it is the small, practical things are important, not so much in themselves, but because they help give expression to this love. They communicate an awareness of that person and a desire to help. Knowing one is cared for in this way can be a great comfort.

Of course, this is often easier said than done. We can notice ourselves adopting all sorts of strategies which in part come out of a desire to help, but are also influenced by our difficulty in being there with that pain. We just want it to go away, so we try to help in a way that does not really take in the person. We start advising them what they need to do about their problem, or immediately respond with a story of how a similar thing once happened to us, or explain our theory of what is going on, or attempt to console them by saying how awful it must be. Yet what is called for is just trying to listen with as full and kind attention as we can muster. We try to really be there with them, without needing to advise, explain, respond, or console the problem away. This is not easy and we may find ourselves having to go back to developing more emotional resources as described above.

I once heard a story that tells us something of what it means to really listen and empathize. The man who told me this story was, as a young boy, in hospital for an operation. This was in the days before special children's wards, so he was in a ward with adult men, which he found rather frightening. But one day he saw an angel outside the window opposite his bed. The angel was beautiful and comforting to see. However, when he told grown-ups that he'd seen an angel, nobody believed him, and he found this upsetting.

Later in life, he found that this incident was quite symbolic for him. He'd often felt not listened to, not taken seriously. This story epitomized how he felt about that. So he would sometimes relate the story as a way of explaining this to others. People would usually be very sympathetic and say things like, 'Oh dear, it must have been really awful not to have been believed.'

But he once told the story and got a different response – the one that, in a way, he'd been waiting for. He told the story to a man who looked more and more interested as he spoke, and afterwards the man leaned forward, his eyes shining with fascination, and said, 'Tell me – the angel – what did it look like?'

exercise – *cultivating compassion*
Looking back over the three points above, what are your strengths and weaknesses?

Can you see ways in which you might learn to distinguish spheres of influence and concern, develop inner robustness and positivity, and develop empathy?

These are all big areas in themselves, so, after reviewing this issue as a whole, you might want to focus on one aspect of it. Just look for one thing that you could bear in mind and practise over the following days and weeks.

The Buddhist tradition has specific meditation practices designed to help us. For example, we can do the loving-kindness practice (described in Chapter 3) by putting in each stage people who we know are suffering. In this way, we try to learn how to come into a compassionate relationship with suffering in the world.

exercise – *compassion meditation*

1. In your meditation practice over the next week, look specifically at compassion – loving-kindness towards those who are suffering. You could try the meditation suggested just now. In each of the five stages of the loving-kindness practice (yourself, friend, neutral person, difficult person, everyone) you become particularly aware of difficulty in people's lives, or you choose people you know who suffer in some way.

2. Watch your own inner responses, trying to soften and relax when you notice yourself tightening, physically or emotionally, in order to exclude pain and suffering. Try sending healing light or warmth to others as you breathe out.

3. Just take the practice as far as you are able and don't give yourself a hard time if you find it difficult. If you find we get overwhelmed by the suffering you are contemplating, it is important to come back to developing inner positivity through, for example, reflection on the good things in life, your own good fortune, and the good that many people do in the world. Maintain a sense of perspective and equanimity.

There is a story about how, when the Buddha was dying, his close friend Ananda was lamenting. He wept and remarked that the Buddha was going away from them, 'he who was so kind'. It is significant that it was *kindness* that Ananda best remembered the Buddha for, not his profound teachings, or skill in debate, or his ability to dwell in deep states of meditation. Maybe we, too, have this same sense to some extent: that nothing in life matters much if we do not have ordinary human kindness. Even all the Buddhist teachings, practices, and so on, are not much use if they do not lead to this. This is what I learn as I travel along the Buddhist path: what I really want, most of all, is just to be able to be more kind.

We will all encounter opportunities to practise kindness and compassion. They present themselves to us every day. We do not know when they might arise. All we need is enough awareness to notice them, and the courage to act.

There will be small ways we can help make the world more human, and there may be big ways too. If we practise acting with small acts of kindness, we are more prepared when the bigger opportunities come along. You could almost say that if we take care of the small opportunities, the larger ones will take care of themselves. We will know what to do. Through what we have developed in the course of our Buddhist life, we will have a deep enough understanding, and a big enough heart.

12

death and rebirth

what happens next

When death comes
like the hungry bear in autumn;
when death comes and takes all the bright coins from his purse...

I want to step through the door full of curiosity, wondering:
what is it going to be like, that cottage of darkness?[34]

The first time I saw a dead person close up was when I was helping organize a funeral at our Buddhist centre. At Buddhist funerals the lid is usually left off the coffin in order that the body can be seen. When the coffin arrived, we lifted it into the shrine room and began to unscrew the lid. I was quite nervous. How would I react to seeing a dead body? Would I feel faint and nauseous, or frightened?

When we lifted off the lid and saw the body lying there, it was simply a relief. It was all so natural and normal. It was only our friend's dead body. He was still recognizable as the friend we knew and loved, but different too. Because it looked so much like him, I somehow expected him to move, or at least shift position. I half-anticipated a flicker of the eyelids, or the gentle rise and fall of the breath. But the more I looked, the more the total stillness and inertness of the body struck me. Something had simply gone.

During the funeral some people were upset. Our friend had been healthy and died unexpectedly in the prime of life, and we were going to miss him. But there was also such a strong expression of love that it was almost a joyful atmosphere too. Friends told stories about him, we

158

placed gifts and cards in the coffin and said our goodbyes. The funeral was for him, but it was also a reminder to us all of our own mortality, and of the uncertainty about when our own death would come.

What is the Buddhist view of what happens to us when we die? In this chapter we will look at the traditional Buddhist teaching of rebirth. According to this, after we die a future life is reborn that is, in some way, linked to ours. This life then gives rise to another life in the future, and so on. But do we have to accept this traditional view in order to be a Buddhist, or to live a Buddhist way of life? We might be deeply attracted to many of the principles and practices of Buddhism, but less sure about the idea of rebirth. We live in a culture that is strongly materialistic and sceptical about the possibility of any form of life after death. The prevailing views of our culture are bound to influence our outlook. We'll explore a range of ways in which western Buddhists might approach the teaching of rebirth.

death and rebirth
As we've already seen, the traditional Buddhist teaching is that of rebirth, or 're-becoming'. A customary image for this is a candle that is alight, but burning low. Soon it will be spent, but the flame can be used to light another candle. Something is passed from flame to flame, though it is hard to say exactly what. Let's look at this idea in more detail.

What we think of as 'me' is actually a complex, interconnected, changing process of events and conditions. Part of this process is physical. For example, the body gets nutriment from food and replenishes itself. Another part of the process is the flow of consciousness: one moment of consciousness conditioning the next moment of consciousness all through our lives. We tend to think of our minds and bodies as enduring, solid things, when in fact they are ever-changing processes.

When we die, these processes carry on, but in a radically different way. Our body is buried or cremated, and the elements it is made of break down and return to the earth and the air. Also, the last moments of consciousness in this life create, according to tradition, the conditions for the first moments of consciousness in the next.

This new life will not be 'you', although who they will be does depend on 'you' as you were in this life. The Buddhist idea of karma (which we explored in Chapter 1) is that we constantly create our future through how we think, speak, and act. If I am generous, I naturally tend to be more generous in the future. If I am tightfisted, I create a different habit, one that makes me less likely to behave generously. In other words, the way we live our lives in the present creates a kind of flow, or momentum, into the future. This is what is called karma. Buddhist tradition maintains that this also carries on from one life to the next. Your consciousness sets off another process of consciousness. It sets it off with a particular momentum, a certain direction and force. In this way, karma is transferred from life to life. This is how many Buddhists are able to see Enlightenment not as a goal for this lifetime, but one 'they' will attain in a future life. The momentum of their practice is transferred to the next consciousness, and so on down the line.

The various Buddhist traditions see this process happening in somewhat different ways. Some maintain that the flow of consciousness flows instantly from the moment of death to the next life. Others believe that there is an in-between state in which the consciousness exists before 'choosing' the next life. There is a well-known Tibetan text, popularly known as *The Tibetan Book of the Dead*, which describes a forty-nine-day journey through such an intermediate state. This is seen as a time of great spiritual opportunity, because it is likened to a state of meditation. The mind is not caught up in the concerns of the world, but is free to experience and explore its own nature. If the consciousness on this journey can realize this, the chances of spiritual realization are great. Even if you cannot believe what the text says literally, it is fascinating and strangely uplifting. Its view of death is highly positive. There, too, we 'dwell in possibility'.

exercise – *where did I come from and where am I going?*
The concept of rebirth can be difficult to understand, so here is a thought experiment that might help.

Imagine yourself as you are now, and then imagine yourself when you were ten years old. Bring to mind your physical attributes both in the present and then in the past, and also your life circumstances and your friendships, all that you know about life now and what you knew then.

Now spend some time contemplating particularly all the ways you are a different person from that ten-year-old. For example, do you look different, do you know different things, do you have quite a different understanding of the world, and do you live life differently, and spend time with different people? Apparently the cells of our body are replaced every seven years, so even on a physical level, that ten-year-old simply does not exist any more. You can reflect on the ways in which he or she has gone.

But now you can also consider the continuity between that ten-year-old and yourself. Think of how, although you are, in a sense, different from that ten-year-old, you are also connected to them. When you were ten years old you had certain experiences that made you into a particular kind of eleven-year-old. You then had experiences that made you into a particular twelve-year-old rather than someone different. And this process of growing, evolving, and conditioning carried on until you arrive at you as you are today. So, in your imagination, you can trace your life-story and try to recall 'you' at various stages between the ten-year-old and you as you are now.

You are not the same as that ten-year-old, but you are connected to them. You are not the same as them, but, because you were like *that* then, you are like *this* now. Life is a flow. It is not a thing, but an activity. We are human *beings*: verbs, as it were, not nouns.

This process will continue into the future. You will go on evolving into a new being until you die. When you die, another kind of evolution occurs and another kind of being is brought into existence. Like the ten-year-old, they will not be the same as you are now, but they will be connected to you in some way.

We can look into this rather mysterious process more deeply. Buddhism is saying that you can describe reality as progression and continuity: the ten-year-old evolves into who you are today. But you can also describe it in terms of change and discontinuity: you and the ten-year-old are quite different. There is both continuity and discontinuity at the same time. Both descriptions are true, but neither captures by itself the whole picture of what is going on.

However, owing to our conditioning and temperament, we might tend to view this process one-sidedly. We might see that there is continuity, and tend to ignore, or gloss over, the discontinuity. This view of the world is called eternalism – an attitude, hope, or predisposition to see things as carrying on, and not to see that they are always changing. We want to believe in life and permanence, and deny death and decay.

On the other hand, we might see the discontinuity, and tend to ignore, or gloss over, the continuity. This way of viewing the world constitutes nihilism – an attitude, or predisposition, to see things as having a final end, and not to see that there is also progression and evolution. We are inclined to notice only the ceasing of things, and not the ever-present possibility of new life and growth.

Buddhism is sometimes described as a 'middle way'. This expression refers to a position between eternalism and nihilism. The Buddha said that both of these were extremes, that the truth lay somewhere in between – in this mysterious process of progression and change, growth and decay, life and death.

Life is king, and we are but travellers in his realm. As we journey, we continually borrow and give back. We take food from the earth, and drink water from the rivers. We need the warmth of the sun, and the air to breathe. But we only borrow them. They are not ours for long. We are continually giving them back. If we eat and drink, we must also defecate and urinate. If we inhale, we must also exhale. In order for there to be growth, there must also be decay. Life and death are two sides of the same coin. My experience of opening the coffin was unnerving partly because death is often hidden away in our culture.

We do not want to talk about it, or look at it, more than we have to. This accentuates the strangeness of death and makes it seem more unnatural and frightening than it need be. But death is natural. It is part of life.

do buddhists have to believe in rebirth?

Although we might understand the general principle of life as a process, and how things are always, simultaneously, in a state of both growth and decay, we might find it more difficult to accept the traditional Buddhist teachings on exactly how this works. We can see that as one thing dies, it gives rise to something else in turn. It's obvious, for example, that plants and animals die, decay, return to the earth, and become the very material that sustains future plants and animals. But it might be harder to believe that an individual consciousness creates another life in the future.

We might be quite sceptical and questioning of the traditional Buddhist view. It has to be said that there are a number of awkward questions that it struggles to answer. For example, if the teaching of rebirth is true, how can the world's population expand so rapidly?

Or we might reasonably take a more agnostic view. We can't yet know what happens when we die. We can accept that there is a process whereby the present affects the future, but we are unsure exactly how this works. Perhaps the traditional Buddhist account of rebirth might be literally true, or it might be some different process: our lives don't give rise to a future life, but it does affect the future in other ways – through our children, or our life's work, and so on. We might be inclined towards a less definite version of rebirth.

Then again, we might feel more open to the tradition. The idea of rebirth does in some ways make more sense that the alternatives. There is some evidence in its favour, and it is worth noting that all Buddhist traditions have upheld the idea of rebirth, although they have differed on many other points.

We could hold any of these positions honestly and reasonably. Perhaps the important thing is to remain open-minded to some extent.

Death, in the end, is a mystery. We do not know where we go, or what happens when we go through that door. How can we possibly know? Even if we had memories of our past lives, there could be other plausible explanations of these. They could be stories we've unconsciously adopted from films or books, or the content of our unconscious working itself out as it does in dreams. The truth is that we cannot know, but we may intuit something. We can have meditation experiences that give us a sense of the possibility of consciousness without the body, or of what consciousness would be like free from attachment to that body. This, again, is not proof, but the experiences may still be significant to us, giving us a sense of openness to the possibilities, and curiosity about what will be.[35]

The Buddha would not answer the unanswerable question of what happens to an Enlightened being after death. He said that none of the categories fitted: one could not say whether he or she would carry on existing, or stop existing, or both, or neither. However, he always insisted that he did not teach nihilism. He was adamant about this when accused of it by rival teachers.

There is another well-known teaching by the Buddha that is a bit like an optimistic, Buddhist version of Pascal's Wager. The Buddha explained that if you believe in rebirth, then it made sense to follow the spiritual path, because then you would gain a good rebirth and work your way towards Enlightenment. If you were wrong about rebirth, it wouldn't matter, because you would still have used your one life to best effect. On the other hand, if you did not believe in rebirth, it was still worth practising. This meant you would make the most of this life and its opportunities. And if you turned out to be wrong, and there was rebirth, you would have done what you needed to best prepare for the next life.[36]

In other words, you don't have to have a definite belief in rebirth in order to practise as a Buddhist. Religion in the West has tended to emphasize *belief*: it is adherence to a creed that defines someone as belonging to a particular faith. But religions in the East have tended to emphasize *practice*: it is what you *do* that is defining and essential.

Of course, this does not mean that belief is entirely unimportant. Our beliefs are related to our deeper attitudes and dispositions. What we believe will affect how we are motivated in the world. For example, if we were a deeply convinced materialist, believing that human beings are just physical organisms that die and have no further significance, we might approach life as a short-lived opportunity to grasp as much pleasure as possible, with little concern for long term considerations.

However, I've known quite a few materialists who don't view life like this. It is not such a simple matter. Our views contain many variations and shades of subtlety. Many of those seemingly staunch materialists I've known have been kinder, more ethical, and more deeply concerned for the welfare of the world than some 'religious' people. Perhaps, although they view their own life as finite, they also have a deeper sense of other lives continuing beyond theirs.

So we come back to the idea that it is not having a definite belief about rebirth that is important, but how we are motivated to live our lives. What we *do* now is more important than what we *think* might happen in the future. What really matters is whether we are making the most of our lives, and doing what we can to create the best future for ourselves and for others.

how we live and how we die

The scriptures that record the stories and teachings of the Buddha are extensive, but they contain surprisingly little factual detail about his life: where he went and whom he met. The emphasis is on certain key incidents and on his teachings. However, it is interesting that the scriptures describing his last days are an exception to this.[37] These do give a detailed chronology. It is as though the Buddha's followers who compiled the scriptures were particularly interested in how he approached death. The way he died was a teaching for them.

It seems that when the Buddha was elderly, the society in which he lived was going through rapid social, political, and economic changes. Old tribal republics were on the wane, and powerful new monarchical kingdoms were on the rise, with the ability to raise armies and extend their territories. There were wars, insurgencies, and corruption, and some of this detail makes its way into the Buddhist scriptures. It provides a poignant and rather grim backdrop to the last days of the Buddha's life. The Buddha had tried to intervene to prevent some of these conflicts, but without success. We even read that an old friend of his, King Pasenadi, is deposed whilst visiting the Buddha, and died of exhaustion just outside the city where he had hoped to find support.[38]

The Buddha had spent all his life teaching and establishing a community of practitioners. This had expanded numerically and geographically. There were now many members of the order who had never met the Buddha and would never do so. He probably felt his influence declining, but he knew that he had done what he could, and the only thing left for him to do was to let go.

So he and Ananda, his companion for twenty-five years, went on one final tour. They visited old haunts and old friends to say their farewells. Then they wandered off into quieter, lesser-known towns and regions. It was almost as though they wanted peace and quiet, and to get away from it all. They had recently received the news that two of the chief followers of the Buddha had died. Their generation was all passing on, and they were two old men alone.

They reached a small town called Kusinara, and, in a nearby grove of sal trees, the Buddha lay down and told Ananda that he would die there. Ananda wanted to know why he had chosen such an insignificant place. Why not go to one of the cities that were large, influential centres of Buddhist activity? But the Buddha told him a story. He said that there once was a great city, right there at Kusinara, but that city and all its grandeur had now gone.

Maybe this, and the earlier backdrop to the story, has a symbolic significance. We are shown a picture of the world carrying on as usual: gain and loss, victory and defeat, rise and fall. The Buddha has lived his life working to improve this society, but he also knows that in themselves worldly things are futile. We cannot hold on to them; they fall away from us, and us from them. To us, this may seem tragic and poignant, but the Buddha just knew that this is the way things are. He was not caught up with the world; he identified with, and saw, a bigger picture.

Ananda is deeply upset that the Buddha is dying and moves away, weeping bitterly. The Buddha notices his absence and asks another monk to fetch him. He tells Ananda that he has always taught impermanence – that everything that is dear to us, we must one day be parted from. He asks Ananda to remember this teaching, and then he sings Ananda's praises to the other monks. He tells them how well Ananda has looked after him all these years, what a good friend he has been, and how well loved and popular with other monks Ananda is. Even in his final moments, the Buddha is aware of, and attending to, the needs of others.

Finally, he tells them, 'be islands to yourselves.' They mustn't rely on him, as he will soon be gone. They must live the life of practice and look to their own experience, gain their own understandings. Then he calmly goes into deep meditation and passes away.

The Buddha presents an example of someone dying fearlessly and at peace with himself. We come back to the idea that what counts is what we make of our lives, how we dwell in the possibilities that it offers. If we live a life of curiosity, then, when death comes, we will be able to go through that door full of curiosity too. If, when we get to the end, we can be satisfied that we did our best, we will go through the door content, rather than with regret. If we have tried to be creative with what life has dealt us, we will not have a sense of missed opportunity. The philosopher Wittgenstein said on his deathbed, 'Tell them I've had a wonderful life.' This is striking, because he certainly did not have an *easy* life. A few years ago, a friend of mine looked after a friend of his who was dying of cancer. He said that in his last few weeks this friend was more alive than he had ever known him. I hope that is how I am able to go when I reach the end of my days.

13

following the path
coming home

I dwell in Possibility –
A fairer House than Prose –
More numerous of Windows –
Superior – for Doors –

Of Chambers as the Cedars –
Impregnable of Eye –
And for an Everlasting Roof
The Gambrels of the Sky –

Of Visitors – the fairest –
For occupation – This
The spreading wide my narrow Hands
To gather Paradise –[39]

The Buddhist way of life is one that works cumulatively; it is the project of a lifetime. With effort, over time, and with the experience that life brings us, we will gradually grow in awareness and loving-kindness, in wisdom and compassion. Our inner practice provides the perspective and inspiration to make our outer activity more creative. This outer work provides the working material for our inner practice. And so the path goes on.

what is enlightenment?
One way this process could be described is as a growth and development of consciousness. Through meditating, being ethical, reflecting,

and being open and creative, we are developing a consciousness, or awareness, that is clearer and more perceptive, expansive and warm, wise and understanding. Our consciousness eventually grows to the extent that we are just as concerned for others as for ourselves. The way we see and understand the nature of the world means that the experience of our self, and our relationship to other people, is very different from our old, egocentric point of view.

In other words, we develop a new kind of consciousness, or enable it to emerge within us. Buddhist traditions have described this more enlightened kind of consciousness in various ways. It can, for example, be spoken of as an awareness that is beyond subject and object. Our minds no longer endlessly split all our experience into one or other of two categories: me and not-me, or mine and not-mine. Instead, we experience the interconnected flow of all things; we are part of everything else, and everything is part of us. This is not just an idea we have, but a deeply felt reality. It is how we perceive the world, and it is on this basis that we respond to the world. It is part of the structure of our whole being.

The Enlightenment, or Awakening, of a Buddha occurs when such a consciousness is fully developed and perfected. A Buddha always has this kind of awareness, and will unfailingly act from it. However, most traditions also describe a particular stage along the way to Enlightenment: a point at which this consciousness is first experienced, or first flickers into being. The different traditions vary in the detail of exactly when and how this happens. Perhaps this illustrates that human beings differ and there are diverse ways in which this experience can occur.

There are stories and teachings that show this first flickering of new consciousness taking place in crisis situations, and also ordinary human moments. It might be the result of a sudden breakthrough, or a gradual deepening of understanding. Perhaps you are deeply struck by the experience as it happens, or perhaps you hardly notice it and don't realize its full significance until later. It can happen deep within meditation, in the midst of an everyday activity, or while helping

169

another human being. You may have just a quick glimpse of it, or a longer lasting and deeper experience.

Whichever way it occurs, such stories also often have a common theme. The person to whom this happens might just smile or laugh. Maybe this is the culmination of a lifetime's work, they have striven for years for this, but, when it comes, it is strangely familiar. It seems so obvious; how could they have missed it for all those years? It feels like coming home. It is what, deep down, they have known all their life. It is what they have always felt to be true. What a relief to have finally come home.

faith and belief

How can we tell if such stories are true? How can we be sure if such expanded states of consciousness are really possible? How do we even know if the Buddha was Enlightened, or that Enlightenment even exists?

As we saw in the previous chapter, Buddhist practice is more about what we do than what we believe. Belief is not unimportant, since there is often a relationship between our beliefs, the way they cause us to see the world, and, consequently, the way we act. But there is no use in holding on to a belief in blind faith. Beliefs held in this way cannot really go deep enough to sustain us on the path. What we need to do is test these ideas in practice and see whether they work for us, or whether they are true to our experience.

In other words, we don't have to put our hands on our hearts and affirm that we are totally convinced that Enlightenment exists, when we don't yet know. But neither does it mean we need to be entirely agnostic, or neutral. Even if we can't finally prove something until we experience it for ourselves, we can still weigh things up, come to a considered opinion, and act accordingly. We might not yet have arrived at a final conclusion, but we can have a provisional, interim position from which we are able to explore further.

For example, as a result of meditation we may start to experience ourselves changing and growing in awareness and loving-kindness. We can ask ourselves why, if we can change that much, can we not change even more – and carry on changing? Why should there be a sudden ceiling on the possibilities of human development? So for us, Enlightenment becomes at least a theoretical possibility.

There are many stories and teachings from the Buddhist tradition that do seem to have an internal consistency to them. There does seem to be a real experience to which they are all pointing. The teachings about the nature of reality might seem to make sense to us rationally, so we might decide it is worth testing and exploring further.

We may also have an intuition. On a heart, or gut, level we just respond to the ideal of wisdom and compassion. We might find it difficult to put our reasons into words, but we sense that this ideal is something of true value, something truly worth striving for.

So although we are not completely certain, we still have a conviction, a confidence, that it is worth pursuing further. The Buddhist word usually translated as 'faith' is *sraddha*, which comes from a root that means 'to place the heart upon'. We can place the heart upon the ideal of Enlightenment because it makes most sense, seems the most human thing to do, the most beautiful ideal we have come across, that which speaks to us most deeply.

the winding path

And so we carry on following the path. If this truth does really exist, we want to find it. We want to try it out and test it for ourselves. We keep up the search for truth, continue in the life of enquiry into the mystery, and we carry on asking questions, seeking for the best way to live. Perhaps, as we go on in this way, our experience confirms the path for us, so our faith may grow stronger. In a strange way, we can become more confident of the goal, but also less concerned about it. We are living the life anyway. Developing awareness and loving-kindness is just what we do. It is what we are about, and we almost don't need to ask why any more. The search is life. It has its own value.

But the spiritual life is not easy. Along the way there are many stages and hurdles. Only gradually do we get to know and understand ourselves. This is partly because the person we are trying to get to know is complex, and always changing. Understanding the different aspects of ourselves, and how they all go together, takes time. Some of those sides to our personalities will not be at all interested in pursuing the path, and they will resist. With experience, we learn how to approach practice in a balanced way that takes these different sides of ourselves into account, gradually bringing them along and including them on the journey. There will be deep and pervasive habits to over-come – habits we've spent a lifetime reinforcing and which won't want to change overnight. There will be times when we realize that our practice has become one-sided. Perhaps we have become too wil-ful in our approach, or too easygoing. We will make mistakes, go down a wrong path, or misunderstand some aspect of the teaching.

We will gradually have to test and develop a way to practise that works for us. It needs to be appropriate to our circumstances, and suit-able for our temperament. In striving to reach the goal we have set ourselves, we will have phases of working hard to change old habits and develop new ones. There will be other phases when it seems more appropriate just to let go and allow new qualities to emerge from within.

It is not a nice, straight, flat road from here to Enlightenment, with clear signposts and lots of breaks at service stations along the way. It is more like a twisty, rocky path through forests and up mountains. There will probably be times when you lose sight of the path altogether, although you can always find your way back on to it.

You'll never know what would have happened had you taken a dif-ferent path. We can never go back and test how it would have been if, at a certain point, we'd taken another turning. There is that famous poem by Robert Frost, *The Road Not Taken*, in which, having taken the less well-worn path, he reflects in his melancholy way how he will never know where the other path led.

Two roads diverged in a wood, and I –
I took the one less traveled by,
And that has made all the difference.[40]

If we are lost in the forest and confronted by a number of different paths, we have to act on the basis of what we know, and choose one path to follow. We have to make a choice; not to choose is a decision that will have consequences. So we make our best decision and then deal as best we can with the situations this brings about. We might find we took a wrong path, but at least we can learn from this about future choices. Failure is not the real problem; it is the fear of failure that prevents us ever committing ourselves to a course of action, or inclines us to deny when we've made a mistake. If we overcome this fear, we may make mistakes, but we can always learn from them.

The farther on we go, the more we learn, and the deeper intuition we develop about where we are going and which turnings to take. We know our sense of direction, we know our true purpose, so we don't have to spend time wistfully wondering where those other routes might have taken us.

The path will not be easy. However, every once in a while we will come to a high clearing and be able to look back. We'll be able to see how far we have come, and we will be able to catch a glimpse of the beautiful mountain we wish to climb.

The sense of 'coming home' is felt at other levels, at other stages along the way. I've known people who had that sensation the very first time they meditated. They immediately knew that what they were doing was vital and natural to them. For others, it might take a lot longer. We must feel free to test the teachings and practices for ourselves and come to our own decision about whether they work for us. Everyone's path is unique.

When we feel we have come home, when we realize this path is the one we wish to tread, we might want to make our commitment to following it more explicit. The value of making such a commitment conscious in this way is that we can be more fully engaged in our journey and less inclined to hold back. Again, it is not that we have come to final conclusions. It is more that there is still a mystery to solve, but we know that we want our lives to be about trying to solve it. We want to give our best to this adventure. We have come to a turning point where we realize this is what holds most meaning for us. There is no formula for how and when this occurs, no set pattern to which we can conform, but perhaps we can know and trust when such a time has arrived.

Many Buddhist traditions have a way – a ceremony or ritual – that allows us to express this commitment. In the Buddhist movement that I am part of, this is called becoming a *mitra*. The word means 'friend', and if and when someone feels ready, they can take part in a simple ceremony in which they offer a flower, a candle, and some incense to the Buddha on the shrine. In doing this they are stating that they consider themselves Buddhists, that Buddhism is the vision of human enlightenment that expresses most clearly and deeply for them what life is about. They are also declaring that they want to do their best to move towards this enlightenment in their own lives – by meditating, practising ethics, or going on retreat. And they are saying that they wish to be part of this particular sangha or community of practitioners. The value of having such a ceremony is that it makes our intention more explicit, and by so doing, strengthens that resolve and changes us further. It inspires us, and others, seeing us make a commitment, are also inspired.

There are a lot of problems in our world, but we are also incredibly fortunate – especially in the developed world. Here, at least, there is usually peace and prosperity. Most of us have good health and expect to live a long life. We have access to education and culture. We are inheritors of so much richness and beauty. Life is comfortable and luxurious for many people. The Buddhist path gives us a vision and some practical tools for making the most of all this. What we need to do is realize our great good fortune, dwell in the possibilities afforded us, live a fully creative life, and also, where possible, make a better world for others.

What we 'come home' to is this sense of possibility. We rediscover ourselves, who we really are, what we really have to offer.

Quite early in my practice of the Buddhist life, I had a dream in which I was far out at sea. The sea had a gentle swell to it, and I felt myself swirling about in the deep water. In the distance I could see land, and I started to swim towards it. It was hard work, but the waves seemed to wash me gently in that direction.

Strangely, I had exactly the same dream the following night, except that this time I was a little nearer towards shore. The same dream occurred yet again and I was still swimming towards the coastline. Each night I found myself closer to land. The waves grew bigger, but this meant they pulled me along more strongly.

On the fifth night, I had one final dream in which I finally walked onto the shore. Then, in the way these things can happen in dreams, my old self just fell away from me, like an old skin. My new self stood in the sunlight and walked across the sparkling sand. I suddenly found myself with a companion. Together we walked up the beach, climbed a cliff, looked back over the ocean, and gazed at the vast deep blue sea.

notes and references

1 Excerpt from Kathleen Raine, 'The Moment', *Selected Poems*, Golgonooza Press, 2000, p.22.

2 Jack Kornfield, *After the Ecstasy, the Laundry: How the Heart Grows Wise on the Spiritual Path*, Rider, 2000, Chapter 1.

3 Reginald Ray, *Indestructible Truth: The Living Spirituality of Tibetan Buddhism*, Shambhala Publications, 2000.

4 My renderings of the four reminders have been strongly influenced by Vishvapani's in *Madhyamavani*, vol.8, Spring 2003 (privately published).

5 *Mahasaccaka Sutta, Majjhima Nikaya 36.*

6 This is not a book about meditation technique. There are books and CDs that explain in detail how to meditate, or, better still, you can learn at a Buddhist centre or class. Recommended books include Paramananda, *Change Your Mind: A Practical Guide to Buddhist Meditation*, Windhorse Publications, 1996, and Kamalashila, *Meditation: The Buddhist Way of Tranquillity and Insight*, Windhorse Publications, 1996. You could also try the website www.wildmind.org

7 Buddhadasa Bhikkhu, *Mindfulness With Breathing: A Manual for Serious Beginners*, Wisdom Publications, 1997.

8 Thich Nhat Hanh, *Miracle of Mindfulness: A Manual on Meditation*, Rider, 1991. This is a classic book on the practice of mindfulness in daily life.

9 Nyanaponika Thera, *The Heart of Buddhist Meditation*, Rider and Company, 1983.

10 Sangharakshita, *Peace Is a Fire: A Collection of Writings and Sayings*, Windhorse Publications, 1995, p.83.

11 Excerpt from William Blake, 'For the Sexes – The Gate of Paradise' in *Blake Complete Writings*, edited by Geoffrey Keynes, Oxford University Press, 1972, p.761.

12 Patrul Rimpoche, quoting 'The Sutra of the Wise and the Foolish', in *The Words of My Perfect Teacher*, Harper Collins, 1994, pp.123–4.

13 Excerpt from William Blake, 'Auguries of Innocence' in *Blake Complete Writings*, op. cit., p.432.

14 Karen Armstrong, 'Ecstasy Gone Awry', *Guardian*, 23 May 2003.

15 Burton Watson (trans.), *Ryokan, Zen Monk-Poet of Japan*, Columbia University Press, 1977, p.35.

16 Anne Donovan, *Buddha Da*, Canongate, 2002.

17 Hakuin's 'Orategama', in Philip Yampolsky (trans.), *The Zen Master Hakuin – Selected Writings*, Columbia University Press, 1971, pp.29ff.

18 Sangharakshita, *Peace Is a Fire: A Collection of Writings and Sayings*, op. cit., p.39.

19 Excerpt from William Blake, 'Auguries of Innocence', in *Blake Complete Writings*, op. cit., p.432.

20 The poem is by the Chinese monk-poet Han Shan. I cannot determine the source this translation, but another translation and more about Han Shan can be found in *The Collected Songs of Cold Mountain (Han Shan)*, translated by Red Pine, Copper Canyon Press, 2000.

21 The Quarrel at Kosambi, *Vinaya Mahavagga* 10.

22 For much more on the meaning of sangha, see Sangharakshita, *What is the Sangha? The Nature of Spiritual Community*, Windhorse Publications, 2000.

23 Rainer Maria Rilke, 'Archaic Torso of Apollo' in *Rilke: The Rose Window and Other Verse from New Poems*, Bullfinch Press, 1977, p.87.

24 This statue is on display at the Birmingham Museum and Art Gallery.

25 The distinction between logos and mythos is drawn out by Karen Armstrong in *The Battle for God: Fundamentalism in Judaism, Christianity, and Islam*, Harper Collins, 2004.

26 I would highly recommend the introduction to the different Buddha figures and visualization practices in Vessantara, *A Guide to the Buddhas; A Guide to the Bodhisattvas; A Guide to the Deities of the Tantra*, Windhorse Publications, 2008.

27 For much more on Buddhist ritual and a detailed introduction to the text of one particular devotional ritual, or puja, see Sangharakshita, *Ritual and Devotion in Buddhism*, Windhorse Publications, 2000.

28 These methods, and some of the images used to describe them, are taken from Padmavajra, *Listening, Reflecting, Meditating*, Padmaloka Books, 1996.

29 John Armstrong, *The Intimate Philosophy of Art*, Allen Lane, The Penguin Press, 2000, pp.60ff.

30 Keats' oft-quoted remark was made in a letter to George and Thomas Keats, 21 December 1817.

31 Sangharakshita, 'Life is King', in *Complete Poems*, Windhorse Publications, 1995, p.285.

32 Sangharakshita, 'The Unseen Flower', in *Complete Poems*, op. cit., p.95.

33 *Therigatha* 63.

34 Excerpt from Mary Oliver, 'When Death Comes', in *New and Selected Poems*, Beacon Press, 1992, p.10.

35 Here are two recommended books on the topic of rebirth and what happens when we die. The first is on the more sceptical, questioning end of the spectrum of debate about the traditional Buddhist view. The second is confident in the traditional view, but also concerned to present the tradition in a way that is not liable to be mistaken as nihilistic. Nagapriya, *Exploring Karma and Rebirth*, Windhorse Publications, 2004. Lama Shenpen Hookham, *There's More to Dying than Death: A Buddhist Perspective*, Windhorse Publications, 2006.

36 The *Kalama Sutta* (*Anguttara Nikaya* 3.65).

37 The *Mahaparinibbana Sutta* (*Digha Nikaya* 16). See also Karen Armstrong, *Buddha*, Phoenix, 2002, pp.148ff, for her account of the story of the Buddha's last days.

38 From the commentary to the *Dhammacetiya Sutta, Majjhima Nikaya* 89.

39 Emily Dickinson, 'I Dwell in Possibility' in *Art and Wonder: an Illustrated Anthology of Visionary Poetry*, edited by Kate Farrell, Bullfinch Press, 1996, p.8.

40 Excerpt from Robert Frost, 'The Road Not Taken', in *Selected Poems*, Penguin, 1973, p.77.

WINDHORSE PUBLICATIONS

Windhorse Publications is a Buddhist charitable company based in the UK. We place great emphasis on producing books of high quality that are accessible and relevant to those interested in Buddhism at whatever level. We are the main publisher of the works of Sangharakshita, the founder of the Triratna Buddhist Order and Community. Our books draw on the whole range of the Buddhist tradition, including translations of traditional texts, commentaries, books that make links with contemporary culture and ways of life, biographies of Buddhists, and works on meditation.

As a not-for-profit enterprise, we ensure that all surplus income is invested in new books and improved production methods, to better communicate Buddhism in the 21st Century. We welcome donations to help us continue our work – to find out more, go to www.windhorsepublications.com.

The Windhorse is a mythical animal that flies over the earth carrying on its back three precious jewels, bringing these invaluable gifts to all humanity: the Buddha (the 'awakened one') his teaching, and the community of all his followers.

Windhorse Publications
169 Mill Road
Cambridge CB1 3AN
UK
info@windhorsepublications.com

Perseus Distribution
1094 Flex Drive
Jackson TN 38301
USA

Windhorse Books
PO Box 574
Newtown NSW 2042
Australia

THE TRIRATNA BUDDHIST COMMUNITY

Windhorse Publications is a part of the Triratna Buddhist Community, which has more than sixty centres on five continents. Through these centres, members of the Triratna Buddhist Order offer classes in meditation and Buddhism, from an introductory to deeper levels of commitment. Bodywork classes such as yoga, Tai chi, and massage are also taught at many Triratna centres. Members of the Triratna Community run retreat centres around the world, and the Karuna Trust, a UK fundraising charity that supports social welfare projects in the slums and villages of South Asia.

Many Triratna centres have residential spiritual communities and ethical Right Livelihood businesses associated with them. Arts activities are encouraged too, as is the development of strong bonds of friendship between people who share the same ideals. In this way Triratna is developing a unique approach to Buddhism, not simply as a set of techniques, but as a creatively directed way of life for people living in the modern world.

If you would like more information about Triratna please visit www.thebuddhistcentre.com or write to:

London Buddhist Centre
51 Roman Road
London E2 0HU
UK

Aryaloka
14 Heartwood Circle
Newmarket NH 03857
USA

Sydney Buddhist Centre
24 Enmore Road
Sydney NSW 2042
Australia

ALSO BY VAJRAGUPTA

SAILING THE WORLDLY WINDS

A Buddhist Way Through the Ups and Downs of Life

How do we really get on in this world? Tossed around by gain, buffeted by loss, borne aloft by praise, cast down by blame, how can we not be ground under, lose all direction, confidence, and sense of purpose? The Buddha had clear guidance on how to rise above these 'worldly winds', and Vajragupta here opens up for us the Buddha's compassionate yet uncompromising teaching.

Using reflections, exercises and suggestions for daily practice, this book can help you find greater equanimity and perspective in the ups and downs – big and small – of everyday life.

ISBN 9781 9073141 0 0
£8.99 / $14.95 / €10.95
136 pages

THE TRIRATNA STORY

This is the story of Triratna (formerly the FWBO), an international Buddhist movement, from its inception in London to its growth worldwide. It is the story of mistakes made, lessons learnt, and how a Buddhist community was built.

ISBN 9781 899579 9 21
£7.99 / $13.95 / €8.95
224 pages

A GUIDE TO THE BUDDHIST PATH
Third edition
by Sangharakshita

The Buddhist tradition, with its numerous schools and teachings, can understandably feel daunting. Which teachings really matter? How can one begin to practice Buddhism in a systematic way? This can be confusing territory. Without a guide one can easily get dispirited or lost.

Profoundly experienced in Buddhist practice, intimately familiar with its main schools, and founder of the Triratna Buddhist Community, Sangharakshita is the ideal guide. In the third edition of this highly readable anthology he sorts out fact from myth and theory from practice, to reveal the principal ideals and teachings of Buddhism. The result is a reliable and far-reaching guide to this inspiring path.

ISBN 9781 907314 05 6
£16.99 / $23.95 / €19.95
264 pages

CHANGE YOUR MIND
by Paramananda

An accessible and thorough guide, this best-seller introduces two Buddhist meditations and deals imaginatively with practical difficulties, meeting distraction and doubt with determination and humour.

Inspiring, calming and friendly ... If you've always thought meditation might be a good idea, but found other step-by-step guides lacking in spirit, this book could finally get you going. — Here's Health

ISBN 9781 899579 75 4
£9.99 / $13.95 / €12.95
208 pages